CARISBROOKE
Palmam qui meruit ferat.

THE BRITISH ARCHER

OR,

𝕮𝖗𝖆𝖈𝖙𝖘 𝖔𝖓 𝕬𝖗𝖈𝖍𝖊𝖗𝖞,

BY THOMAS HASTINGS
COLLECTOR OF HIS MAJESTY'S CUSTOMS.

The Naval & Military Press Ltd

published in association with

ROYAL ARMOURIES

ROYAL
ARMOURIES

The Library & Archives Department at the Royal Armouries Museum, Leeds, specialises in the history and development of armour and weapons from earliest times to the present day. Material relating to the development of artillery and modern fortifications is held at the Royal Armouries Museum, Fort Nelson.

For further information contact:
Royal Armouries Museum, Library, Armouries Drive,
Leeds, West Yorkshire LS10 1LT
Royal Armouries, Library, Fort Nelson, Down End Road, Fareham PO17 6AN

Or visit the Museum s website at
www.armouries.org.uk

In reprinting in facsimile from the original, any imperfections are inevitably reproduced and the quality may fall short of modern type and cartographic standards.

PREFACE.

To revive an interest in the delightful pastime of Archery, and to encourage the practice of an art which promises health, pleasure satisfaction, and applause, is the aim of the present undertaking.

Archery requires only to be more generally known, and rendered familiar, to become universally adopted and esteemed.

Much of the present Work, has been extracted from rare and expensive publications. The Author has endeavoured to compress the most valuable information on the subject, and to keep alive that interest which it is calculated to excite ; and he hopes that his efforts may tend to raise a desire of becoming acquainted with so charming a recreation, as that which is to be found in the practice of that NOBLE INSTRUMENT, THE BOW.

Archery, the great security and bulwark of our Ancestors, naturally occupies a place of great interest in the minds of Englishmen, and for the services which the Bow has rendered to this Country, it must ever be held in grateful remembrance.

The Bow, is of remote antiquity, and hath been the most common of all Weapons. It is uniformly mentioned in the Sacred Volume as an Instrument generally used by the Jews in their Wars and Conflicts. It not only afforded protection, from an invading foe, and in predatory warfare, but was the chief means by which both food and raiment were procured. By this Weapon, the greatest conquests and victories have been achieved, and through its particular assistance, the less numerous have often been enabled to withstand the utmost force of the mightiest Empires.

Antique Sculpture, and the fables of the Greeks testify, that the Bow was held in high regard by that people.

Among the Persians, and the more eastern Nations, this instrument was, for a series of years quite revered, and even to this day, notwithstanding the introduction of fire-arms, it is greatly prized.

Moseley, in his excellent work on Archery, records, that in the East, the bow gained a hieroglyphical figure, and was represented as a King, and the arrow as an Ambassador.

War, always was, (and it still continues to be,) the chief art cultivated, among even the most civilized nations. It was therefore natural, that the bow, which, in its effects, was found useful in the constant war which man waged against the beasts of the field, should afterwards be turned to the destruction of the human race.

Its first use gained for it an universal reception and confidence, its latter, assigned it the chief place among implements of war, long after the introduction of gun-powder.*

The various accounts which we have of the effects of the English Long-Bow in battle, are quite surprising; and, but for their being so well authenticated, we should at this day, be inclined to treat them with a smile of unbelief, as "*Long-bow stories,*" because we have no adequate means of forming a just estimation of them.

The victories obtained by the ancient English Archers over their enemies, were many and glorious, they are their best Eulogies, and stand upon record in the histories of this country, for the perusal and for the admiration of posterity.

The Bow, that "*ancient Weapon of renown,*" has completed for us the task it was destined to accomplish, and we have *now*, to look upon it only as an Instrument capable of affording much excellent amusement.

To those who are partial to the art of Archery, and who pursue it with that animation which it deserves, the Bow readily proves a source of health and strength, and consequently a helpmate to all the enjoyments of life.

* Roberts. Eng. Bowman.

ON THE INVENTION OF THE BOW.

MOSELEY, in his essay on Archery, thinks it vain to make conjectures on the probable cause of the invention of the bow, and concludes, because the earlier periods of the world are hidden in such dense obscurity, that we cannot form any plausible hypothesis to serve as an explanation.

Some circumstances however must have given rise to the Bow and Arrow, and as we are in possession of the fact, that this weapon was known in the most distant times, it may not be amiss, to endeavour to draw some conclusion as to the probable mode of the discovery.

The use of the bow may be dated from about that early period which immediately succeeded the fall of man!

The invention of the instrument like most other discoveries, was probably from something which nature presented, either in the whole, or in part.—It is easier however to conceive, that a *combination* of circumstances led to the discovery, than to imagine that the display of any single natural object first attracted attention, and from which we might venture to assimilate its construction.—Among the very earliest people of the earth, no doubt, recourse was soon had to missive weapons. Let it be presumed then that the first means which Man took for self defence, and subsequently for the destruction of his prey, were a stick and a stone.—Throwing the stick would suggest the utility of sharpening one or both ends of it. Here we have the invention of the Spear, or small Dart, useful either in throwing, or, for close contest.

The stone, doubtless was soon found to be an effective missile, and the desire of casting it with greater force than could be given by the arm alone, would naturally at the same time be entertained. In this we perceive the first dawn of the Invention of the Sling ; and as it must have been immediately evident, that in the increased length of a stick, would be produced an additional power or weight of blow, so it would have proved the certainty of throwing the stone with much increased force, by whirling it with a longer instrument than that, which the mere hand and arm afforded. Length and flexibility were wanted, and these deficiencies, it may very reasonably be supposed, were supplied by the intestines of Animals, or the bark of trees, by which, we will also presume, the Sling was formed. Having by these means experienced the efficacy of throwing a stone with a surprising increase of force, the thought probably suggested itself to the early hunter, that the throwing of his small spear or dart with equal strength, would be desirable.

The elasticity of wood must necessarily have been known before the construction of the bow. Trees bending from the effect of wind and recovering themselves, afforded a perpetual example of it, and could hardly have been overlooked.

Let us then place before us some circumstances through which probably it was discovered, that a piece of wood bent, and recovering or disengaging itself, displayed a *casting* power, pointing out the utility of the application of the string.

The primitive huts or places of shelter were, most likely, constructed in a manner similar to that which is adopted at the present day by Savage Nations, viz.: by bending long stakes, and fixing each end of them in the ground, thereby forming both the ribs and the rafters of their humble dwellings.

Then let us imagine one end of a bent rib, or rafter to break its hold. Being thus freed, Expansion would naturally take place, and the adherent smaller parts of the little building would be forcibly cast away. Such an accident would be sufficient at once, to give a hint for the formation of the bow ; and the application of its powers to propel the rudely formed dart or spear, would soon be discovered.

In some such instance, probably was first displayed the propelling quality which existed in the Combination of the stick and the string.

ON THE IMPROVEMENT OF THE BOW,
FROM ITS FIRST INVENTION.

The first Bows, doubtless, were formed of rough boughs of trees ; and as their value in attack and defence must soon have been proved, the attention of man would immediately have been directed towards the improvement of the weapon.

The simple bough being shaped into a more convenient form, and the utility of making each end more taper than the centre, evident, would have pointed out the advantage of either making the curve of the bow *regular throughout*, or a distinct bend in each Limb of the instrument, i.e. from either side of the handle to the tips ; and shewn, that with regard to proper length, substance, and quality of the material, for the attainment of a sharp and strong cast, more was to be discovered.

The bow probably remained in its *comparatively* rude state, for a length of time.

Different Nations have always had their own peculiar *mode* of making bows, yet the *principles* upon which bows were constructed, were ever similar in all countries.

Among savage people, and a great part of the eastern world, the practice of using reed or cane is still common. In the days of Job, it appears that steel was used in the construction of the bow.* Homer informs us, that bows were sometimes made of horn; speaking of that of Pandarus, he says,

> " 'Twas form'd of *Horn* and smooth'd with artful toil,
> A mountain Goat † resigned the shining spoil."

And in the Poet's further description of this same Weapon, we may conclude, that the ancients ornamented their bows very highly.

> " The Workmen joined and shaped the bended horns,
> And beaten gold each taper point adorns."

Yew is mentioned by Homer as a bow-wood of the ancients.

The Chinese Tartars, East Indians, Turks, and Persians generally manufacture their bows of wood and horn combined.

Sometimes the Persians make small, but very strong bows of the horns of the Antelope, which are generally much more inflected that any others.

The only Materials hitherto employed, with good effect, in the long bow, have been horn and wood; the former, or both

---

* See chap. xx, verse 24. " He shall flee from the Iron Weapon, and the bow of *steel* shall strike him through."

† The Horns of the Gortynian Goat are often mentioned as bows.

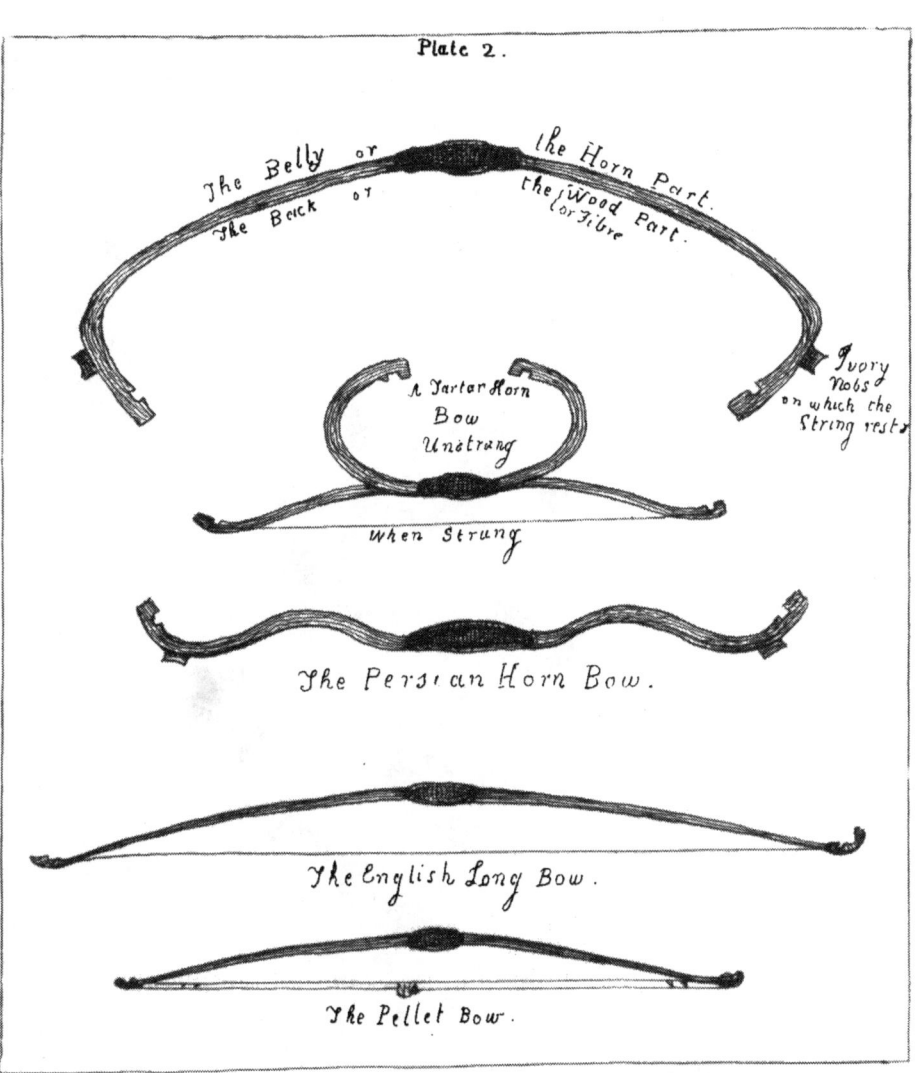

combined, are peculiar to the Eastern, the latter, to most of the European and other Nations. *

It has been imagined that the horn used in the Bows of the Chinese Tartars and others, undergoes the process of liquefaction; but this must be quite erroneous, as by liquefying horn, the substance becomes short and very brittle, and more fit for the manufacture of combs and small fancy work; whereas in the natural state of horn, the fibres which may be perceived to run perfectly from one end to the other, are preserved, and ensure, by their tenacity, that toughness and power of cast which are indispensably necessary. Wood and Sinews form the backs of these Bows and horn the bellies of the Instruments. The backs are covered with fibres, or animal sinews, and upon these, the horn is afterwards fixed by strong glue or cement, and runs from the handle to within 8 or 10 inches of the nocks. The Nocks or Ends of these bows are of wood and most artfully fixed to the Sinews and the Horn, over which sinews and birch bark is cemented.

Chinese Tartary bows, vary in length from about 3 to full 5 feet when bent. The largest, possess prodigious power, and are capable of casting a *light* arrow full five hundred yards. The string is commonly of twisted silk.† These Bows are remarkably pleasant in drawing and will allow of Arrows being pulled to the head, of 33 or 34 inches in length,—nearly the full stretch of a tall man's arm.

* Steel has been lately attempted for the long bow, but without success, for if made strong enough to insure a quick cast, it was found to be far beyond the power of man to draw it without mechanical aid: and when otherwise, it proved extremely sluggish in the cast.

† Strings made of Silk, are necessarily thicker than those manufactured of hemp,—and therefore are not so well calculated for quick casting.

The South Americans, the People of Surinam, and the Africans, have long straight bows of tolerable great strength to this day; particularly the former people, who use them often, as high as 90℔ power. Some of these weapons, are 7 feet in length between the nocks,—and are occasionally made of a most beautiful hard dark wood, called Snake Wood and Copie Wood, and another sort, resembling the finest Mahogany; they bear a remarkably high polish, and although heavy, afford a quick cast.

The backs of American bows are mostly grooved.—In respect to the figures, or length of the various bows made use of in *Ancient* times, we have nothing to shew us but sculptured tradition, or assertions of historians, most of whom, probably were wholly unacquainted with Archery.

Herodotus says, that the bows used by the Ethiopians, were of Palm Tree, the length not less than 4 cubits* and that these people shot with extremely long arrows.

The Carducian bow was, (according to Moseley,) 3 cubits long, and the arrows 2.

During the time of Julius Cæsar, the bow was much in use among the Cretans, whose Archers then composed part of the Roman Troops.†

From this fact, we must conclude, either that the Romans brought the bow to this country, or caused some improvements to be made on those which they found in the possession of the Britons.

---

* The Cubit was a foot and a half of our measure.——The ancient Egyptian cubit was (according to Mr. Graves) one foot nine inches and three quarters of our measure.

† See 2nd book of Julius Cæsar's Commentaries.

Previous to the Norman Conquest, it does not appear that the English paid any particular attention to archery. That great event was doubtless brought about by the superiority of the Norman archers over those of our own Country. The severe lesson that was then taught to the vanquished, was not forgotten. From that period, the English archers began to rise, and prove themselves " terrible in Arms," and not only ultimately to equal, but to excel all the former exploits of other Nations. Thus, it may be said, that Archery became, the Theme of this Kingdom and naturalized to the Country.*

King William encouraged and commanded the practice of the bow, and in a short time after the battle of Hastings, the English archers formed a considerable portion of the National infantry.

The ancient English Long Bows, used as weapons of war, were made of wood only, and the most esteemed were of *foreign* yew.

The superior value of *foreign* Yew as a Bow-wood, is recognised by statutes passed in the reign of Edward IV, and Richard III. which direct, that Bow-staves " shall be imported from Venice ;" † according to Grose, we find that " To prevent a too great consumption of foreign yew, it was enacted, by Act 33, Henry VIII, that Bowyers were to make four bows of any other wood to one of yew," and any person under 17 years of age, (unless possessed of move-

---

* According to Grose, Archery, which during the Reign of Edward the 3rd, was raised to the highest pitch of excellence that most probably it ever attained, was kept up 'till about the year 1643, when it gradually gave way to the use of fire-arms.

† Spanish and Flemish yew was also much esteemed for Bows, and Stow says "that the People of Castile, purposely destroyed their woods, and provided by Law that no such wood should be preserved. The best yew, however, for bows appears unquestionably to have been imported from Venice. In the Reign of Richard III. merchants trading to places from whence bow-staves were commonly brought, were obliged to import four bow-staves for every ton of Malmsey or Tyre wine, under a penalty of 13s. 4d. and in order to encourage the Importation, those of six feet and a half long or more, were excused payment of duty.

ables worth 40 marks, or the son of Parents having an Estate of ten pounds, per annum ;) not to shoot in a *yew* bow, under a penalty of 6s..8d.

The act, 8th. of Elizabeth, Cap. 10th. regulates the prices of bows, and directs, that when "a common, or Livery bow, or a bow of *English* yew, is sold for 2s. a bow of *foreign* yew, may be sold for 6s..8d. It may here be remarked, that Mr. Ainsworth, a Bowyer, living at Walton le Dale near Preston very lately sold two Self Bows made by himself, of *Spanish* Yew, one for £8—the other for £10. The length of English bows during the reign of Edward IV. became a matter for legislative consideration, questionless for the purpose of preventing an apprehended decline of the then hitherto acquired power of English Archery.

On referring to the statute of 5th Edward IV, Cap. iv, we find that "Every Englishman, and Irishman, that dwell with Englishmen and speak English, that be betwixt sixteen and sixty in age, shall have an English bow of his own length, and one fistmele,* *at the least*, betwixt the necks, with 12 Shafts of the length of three quarters of the Standard."

Estimating the breadth of an ordinary man's fist at about four inches, the bow for a man five feet six inches high was by this law required to be nearly six feet betwixt the Nocks; but the Irish Statute of Edward IV. says "That the bow shall not exceed the height of a man," &c.—Judging from the fact, that the common range of an English Archer's shot in these early times, was from sixteen to twenty score yards, we may form some notion of the prodigious power of the bows used by this country in battle, and of the great muscular strength required, to use with effect, such mighty machines.

* "Fistmele" meant handful.

From the well authenticated and undoubted records of the effects of our ancient strong shooting, it would not be overrating the strength of the war bow, to say, that it must have been from 100 to 120 and 150 pounds.*

It would be needless to recount the various acts passed during the successive reigns of the kings of England, for the encouragement of Archery; suffice it to say, that from the days of William the Conqueror, in whose reign, the art attracted the *particular* attention of the Government, to the Sixteenth Century, it was the great security and bulwark of the land.

In the East Indies, and in South America, the natives make use of another sort of Long-bow, called the Pellet-Bow, which is calculated more for shooting small birds, than to be used as an Instrument of attack or defence. It has two strings of equal length, which are kept asunder by a piece of cane about an inch long, at nearly two inches from each extremity of the bow. At the centre of the strings, is a sort of small webbed half-bag, in which the pellet is placed. The missile is held therein, between the finger and thumb; and at the moment of loosing the string, the bow-arm is stretched out, so as to twist the strings a little outwards, which movement allows the pellet to pass without danger to the bow-hand. The pellets are usually made of clay.

From the time that Archery was first introduced into this country, to the days of Henry VIII, the English bow was formed of only one piece of wood. Had it been otherwise, no doubt Ascham would

* Henry VIII. passed acts relative to Archery, and amongst the several rules and regulations made for the support of the art, was one that says, "none under 24 years of age, might shoot any standing mark except it was for a rover, and then he was to change his mark at every shot, under the penalty of four-pence for every shot made contrary, &c. Also, that no person above the age of 24 should shoot at any mark that was not above *eleven score* yards distant, under pain of forfeiting for every shot 6s..8d.

have noticed it in his "Toxophilus."—Since his time, a most important discovery in Archery has been made, by uniting a thin piece of tough and spirited wood, such as ash, hiccory, or lance wood, to the principal part of the bow. Bows of this sort have, since the invention, been called *backed*, and the other sort from that time, received the title of self-bows.—About six years ago, a Mr. J. Dennett, of Newport, in the Isle of Wight, made an experiment by introducing a small slip of quick casting wood along in the centre of the belly of a bow, from the handle to the nocks.—It succeeded admirably.

From the days of the first decline of English archery, the growth of the Bow-woods, particularly that of Yew, has been much neglected; and probably from the consequent difficulty of obtaining an adequate supply of good clean staves, to make *self*-bows, (which should be at least six feet in length,) the idea of backing two shorter pieces of bow-wood to make one whole, was entertained, a notion, which might perhaps have been strengthened by the example already set, in the formation of the bows of the Chinese Tartars, and other Eastern people.*—The invention of backing, has frequently been attended with considerable advantages, not only in enabling a Bowyer to produce a good bow from two distinct pieces of short wood, which otherwise would have been useless, but even in case of a fret, or small crack appearing on the *back* of a valuable Self-bow, when the back or sap of such an instrument might be cut away, and prepared for the reception of a perfect and well seasoned piece of ash, hiccory, or lance wood.

The Art of uniting two pieces of wood in the construction of the bow, has given birth to a further experiment in Archery.

* The Belly part of a backed bow, is generally in two pieces united in the centre, but the wood with which they are backed must be one entire piece, from Nock to Nock.

Bows have been made consisting of three, four, and somtimes five pieces. *

It has been justly remarked, " that had the bow continued a military weapon in this country, it would in all probability, have derived new powers; or at least those which it is acknowledged to possess, would have been increased, by means of that perfection which philosophy and the arts have to this day attained." Possibly the present method of working in, and tempering, horn and steel, might, under the skill of modern artificers, lead to something highly useful to Archery, either by connecting those two materials with wood, or by using them separately and independently. The trial seems worthy the effort of genius, for should it succeed, the bow " the peculiar engine of the land," might again become the superior and all-conquering weapon of war !"

ANECDOTES OF ARCHERY.

THE bow is frequently mentioned in Holy Writ. In the sacred volume, we find that Isaac called his son Esau, and said, "Now therefore take, I pray thee, thy weapons, thy quiver and thy bow,

---

* The manufacturing of these bows, requires great attention. Mr. Waring of London has brought bows of this description to a high perfection. The backed ones which consist only of one or two pieces of wood for the belly, and the second or third or whole piece for the back, are probably sufficiently hazardous, considering the uncertainty and moisture of the English climate, without increasing the chance of separation and fracture by the addition of two more pieces *glued* together—Every backing is necessarily attended with much risk and trouble. The fixing of the several parts together, is done in frames, which are generally reflexed, without which, good backing cannot be accomplished.—Hence the necessity of employing a good Bowyer.

and go out to the field, and take me some venison ; and make me savoury meat, such as I love, and bring it to me, that I may eat, that my soul may bless thee before I die." *

Jonathan, the son of Saul, was a skilful Archer, but it appears that the bow had been neglected amongst the armies of Israel, for in the fatal battle near mount Gilboa, between Saul and the Philistines, we read ; " The battle went sore against Saul, and the archers hit him, and he was sore wounded of the archers." †

In the succeeding chapter, we are told that David gave orders for the children of Judah to be taught the use of the bow.

We find the bow mentioned occasionally by Homer. The Poet speaking of Pandarus aiming an arrow at Menelaus, the action is thus described : ‡

> " Now with full force the yielding horn he bends,
> Drawn to an arch, and joins the doubling ends ;
> Close to the breast he strains the nerve below,
> Till the barb'd point approach the circling bow ;
> Th' impatient weapon wizzes on the wing,
> Sounds the tough horn, and twangs the quivering string."

The Locrians were a body of troops in the Grecian army, who occasionally used both the bow and the sling.§

> " The Locrian squadrons, nor the jav'lin wield,
> Nor bear the helm, nor lift the moony shield ;
> But skill'd from far the flying shaft to wing,
> Or whirl the sounding pebble from the sling.—
> Dext'rous with these they aim a certain wound,
> Or fell the distant warrior to the ground."

* Genesis xxviii, 3, 4. † 1 Samuel xxxi, 3. ‡ Iliad book iv, line 152.
§ Iliad book xiii, line 891.

The suitors of Penelope, having in vain attempted to bend the bow of Ulysses, (that hero being present disguised like a beggar,) he with much difficulty obtains leave to try his skill.

"————————————One hand aloft display'd,
The bending horns, and one the string essay'd.
From his essaying hand the string let fly,
Twang'd short and sharp, like the shrill swallow's cry.
A general horror ran through all the race,
Sunk was each heart, and pale was every face.—
When fierce the hero o'er the threshold strode;
Stript of his rags, he blaz'd out like a god.
Full in their face the lifted bow he bore,
And quiver'd deaths, a formidable store:
Before his feet the rattling shower he threw,
And thus terrific, to the suitor crew;
One vent'rous game this hand has won to day,
Another, Princess! yet remains to play;
Another mark our arrow must attain,
Phœbus! assist; nor be the labour vain.
Swift as the word the parting arrow sings,
And bears thy fate, Antinous, on its wings:
Wretch that he was, of unprophetic soul!
High in his hands he rear'd the golden bowl.
Even then to drain it, lengthen'd out his breath;
Chang'd to the deep, the bitter draught of death:
For fate who fear'd amidst a feastful band!
And fate to numbers, by a single hand!
Full thro' his throat Ulysses' weapon past,
And pierced the neck, He falls, and breathes his last."

Eneas, in celebrating the anniversary of his Father's funeral, amongst other sports and exercises, introduces archery.

"Forthwith Eneas to the sports invites
All who with feathered shafts would try their skill;
And names the prizes. With his ample hand
He from Serestus' ship a mast erects;

And on it by a rope suspended ties
A swift-wing'd dove, at which they all should aim
Their arrows: They assemble; and the lots
Shuffl'd into a brazen casque are thrown.
With fav'ring shouts Hippocoon first appears,
Offspring of Hyrtacus: Then Mnestheus next,
So lately victor in the Naval strife;
And crown'd with olive green, Eurytion third.

* * * * * *

Then all with manly strength
Bend their tough yeugh; each with his utmost force,
All from their quivers draw their shafts: and first
Shot from the twanging nerve, Hippocoon's flies
Along the sky, beats the thin liquid air
And on the body of the mast adverse
Stands fix'd: the mast and frighted bird at once
Tremble, and all the cirque with shouts resounds.
Next eager Mnestheus with his bended bow
Stands ready, and his eyes and arrow aim'd
Direct to heav'n; yet could not reach the dove,
Herself, unfortunate, but cut the knots,
And hempen ligaments in which she hung
Ty'd by the feet upon the lofty mast,
She flies into the winds and dusky clouds.
Eurytion then impatient, and long since
Holding his ready bow and fitted shaft,
Invokes his brother, and in open air,
Seeing the dove now shake her sounding wings,
Transfixes her amidst the clouds: the bird
Falls dead, and leaves her life among the stars!"

After Cambyses had conquered Egypt, he turned his attention to the invasion of Ethiopia, and accordingly sent some spies into that country; under pretence of carrying presents to the king; but he ordered them to enquire privately into the strength and condition of the kingdom.—When they arrived at court, and had made their presents, the king of Ethiopia said to them; "It was not from any consideration of my friendship, that the king of Persia sent you to me with these presents; neither have you spoken the truth, but are come into my kingdom as Spies.—If Cambyses were an honest man, he would desire no more than his own, and not endeavour to reduce a people under servitude, who have never done him any injury. However, give him this bow from me, and let him know, that the king of Ethiopia advises the king of Persia to make war against the Ethiopians, when the Persians shall be able thus easily to draw so strong a bow, and in the meanwhile, to thank the Gods, that they never inspired the Ethiopians with a desire of extending their dominions beyond their own country." Saying this, he unbent the bow, and delivered it to the Ambassador.

The armies of Alexander the Great, were composed chiefly of archers.

The Bowmen of Athens performed wonders in many battles, but particularly under Demosthenes, when they defeated the Lacedemonians near the city of Pylos.—Plato mentions, that one thousand archers were appointed for the standing guard of the city of Athens. This celebrated philosopher was an advocate for archery, and recommended that masters should be employed by the state to teach the Athenian youth the use of the bow.

The Cretans were taught archery at seven years of age; and so expert were this people, that the neighbouring monarchs were desirous of having a band of Cretan archers in their armies.*

---

* In Livy, we read that the Cretan archers completely routed the army of Antiochus, and turned his cavalry into flight " by a *storm of arrows*."

"The arrows of Gortynia, says Claudian,
"Aimed from a trusty bow, are sure to wound,
"Nor ever miss the destined mark."

The victories obtained by the Parthians over the Romans, were chiefly ascribed to their superiority in the use of their bows. With these they pursued Marchus Antoninus over the hills of Media and Armenia, conquered the noble Valerian, and slew the apostate Julian.

Historians frequently mention the torments endured by those who had been wounded by arrows.

"Touching the galling of the enemy," says Clem. Edmonds "there cannot be a better description, than that which Plutarch (Plut. Crassus) maketh of the overthrow of the Romans, by the Parthian Archers. The Roman soldiers' hands were nailed to their targets, and heir feet to the ground, or otherwise were sore wounded in their bodies, and died of a cruel lingering death, crying out for the very anguish and pain they felt, and turning and tormenting themselves upon the ground, they break the arrows sticking in them. Again, striving by force to pluck out the barbed heads, that had pierced far into their bodies through their veins and sinews, they opened their wounds wider, and so cast themselves away."*

The page of history points out the fact, that the Romans in the zenith of their power and dominion, though conquerors of Europe, Africa, and the East, could yet make no impression on the monarchy of the Arsacides, but were, for ages, defeated in all their attempts by the Parthian archers.

Xenophon bears testimony to the prodigious force of the bow. In his account of the retreat of the ten thousand Greeks, who sorely

* Lib. 7, c. 15. See also Roberts's English Bowman.

felt the effects of the arrows of the Carducians, he relates: "Here fell a brave man, Cleonymus, a Lacedemonian, who was wounded in the side by an arrow, that made its way both through his shield and buff coat." Again he says; "Here fell Basius, an Arcadian, whose head was quite shot through by an arrow." And Plutarch affirms, that this strong shooting continued among the descendants of the Carducians, till the time of Crassus, whose soldiers were slaughtered by their arrows, in vast numbers, "as no part of their armour could withstand the force of them."

The Alans, Huns, and Dacii, who finally overthrew the empire of the west, were remarkable for archery.

The Arabian tribes, emerging from their confined and desert territory, established the vast power of the Caliphs by means of the bow. After them, the Turks overthrew the eastern empire by the same weapon.

Archery was cultivated by many private individuals of the Roman state.

The Circus was often the scene where feats of archery were exhibited, and even emperors themselves were actors.

Domitian and Commodus, were particularly celebrated for their matchless excellence in the use of the bow.

The feats of Commodus were numerous. He was one of the most expert archers that ever lived. Many stags, lions, panthers, and other species of beasts, fell by his hand. It is said that a *second* arrow was never necessary! He would strike an animal in any particular point he wished, with the greatest accuracy. A panther was sometimes let loose into the circus, where a criminal was placed, and just as the animal was going to seize the culprit, he would drive an arrow so opportunely, that the man should escape unhurt.* One hundred beasts have been introduced at the same time upon the arena, and with the same number of shafts, he would lay them lifeless.

The Persians appear, from all accounts, to be astonishingly expert in the art of shooting in the Long-bow. These people may be placed with the first rank of Archers. Chardin says, that the Persians, in their exercises, shoot in the bow with incredible accuracy; so accurate, that "they will often drive an arrow into the same hole." Their excellence, in shooting, while on horse-back, is thus described by Chardin. "A mark is placed on the top of a pole, about twenty-six feet from the ground, the horseman rides at full speed towards the mark, and having passed it, (his bow being ready drawn) turns round, and discharges his arrow backwards. Sometimes they shoot to the right hand, and sometimes to the left." The nobility and kings are fond of, and often practise this amusement.

The exercise of archery among the Persians was, (and probably is to this day,) practised thus; "The young people are taught at an early period to hold the bow firmly, to draw, and to let go the string smoothly. At first, they practise with weak bows, and afterwards by degrees, with others that are stronger. The Instructors in the art, direct their pupils to shoot with ease and agility in every direction;—before them,—behind,—and on either side, elevated in the air, or low to the ground.—When the pupils can manage a common bow, they then have another given to them, and when they understand how to handle the bow well, their first exercise, is to shoot in the air as high as they can. Afterwards, they are taught to shoot point blank. The art of shooting point blank, is not only in hitting

* Herodian makes particular mention of the "unerring hand" of Commodus. Lib. I—15.

the mark, but it is necessary also that the arrow goes firmly and steadily. Lastly, pupils are practised in shooting with very heavy Shafts, and with very great force."

Although among the Turks, the practice of the Bow is not so vigorously pursued as in former times, this Weapon is still retained as an implement of war. According to Sir John Smith, "Vallies ran with rivers of blood, caused by the slaughter from the Turkish Bow."—And Gibbon says, "that the first body of the Crusaders, was overwhelmed by the Turkish arrows, and a pyramid of bones informed their companions of the place of their defeat."

The victory obtained by the Normans over the English, at the battle of Hastings, was the seed sown for the future harvest of English renown, and the early germ of the wreath for British archery.

After the period of the Norman Conquest, archery became an object of the highest consideration to the government of this country. The superior personal strength, added to that cool and steady tempered resolution, so peculiarly natural to our general national character, may be said to have been the help-mates to those great advantages which the English possessed in their archers, and which enabled them continually to gain the most decisive victories, with great disparity of numbers, over every nation with whom they had to contend in arms. With these advantages of heart and strength, the opponents of the English archers were unable to stand against them with any chance of success.

William II., whilst hunting in the New Forest with Sir Walter Tyrrell, was accidentally killed by one of the knight's arrows.

Richard I. of England, when besieging the castle of Chaluze, approached, too near the walls, and was mortally wounded by an arrow. During the reign of this monarch, we first find particular mention made of Robin Hood the celebrated Chief of English Archers. The intestine troubles of England were very great at that time, and the country was much infested with outlaws and banditti, amongst whom, none were so notorious as this "Sylvan Hero" and his followers. Stow, in his annals, styles them "Renowned Thieves."

The personal courage of this celebrated outlaw, his skill in archery, his humanity, and especially his levelling principle, of taking from the rich and giving to the poor, have severally been perpetuated in the *poetical effusions* of the times, and which have served to hand his fame down to posterity, as well as to excite an extraordinary degree of lively interest in every circumstance with which the name of Robin Hood is connected.

Hearne, in his Glossary, inserts a manuscript note of Wood containing a passage cited from John Major, the Scottish historian, to this purpose; that Robin Hood was indeed an arch-robber, but the gentlest thief that ever was: and he remarks, that he might have added from the Harlein MSS. of John Fordun's Scottish Chronicle, that he was, though a notorious robber, a man of great charity.

The true name of Robin Hood was Robert Fitz-ooth.—The addition of "Fitz," common to many Norman names, was afterwards often omitted.

The last two letters "th," being turned into "d," he was called "Ood," or "Hood."—It is evident he was a man of quality, as by the annexed pedigree taken from Dr. Stukeley's "Palæographia Britanniæ." Leland also has expressly termed him "*Nobilis*" (Collectanea I. 54.) from Ritson we read, "Ralph Fitzothes or Fitzooth, a Norman, who had come over to England with William

Rufus, married Maud, or Matilda, Daughter of Gilbert de Gaunt, Earl of Kyme and Lindsey, by whom he had two Sons: Philip, afterwards Earl of Kyme, that Earldom being part of his Mother's dowry, and William. Philip the elder died without issue; William was a ward to Robert de Vere, Earl of Oxford, in whose household he received his education, and who, by the King's express command, gave him in marriage to his own Niece, the youngest of the three daughters of the celebrated Lady Roisia de Vere, Daughter of Aubrey de Vere, Earl of Guisnes in Normandy, and Lord High Chamberlain of England under Henry I. and of Adeliza, Daughter to Richard de Clare, Earl of Clarence and Hereford, by Payn de Beauchamp Baron of Bedford her second husband. The offspring of this marriage was, Robert Fitzooth, commonly called Robin Hood."

THE PEDIGREE OF ROBIN HOOD.

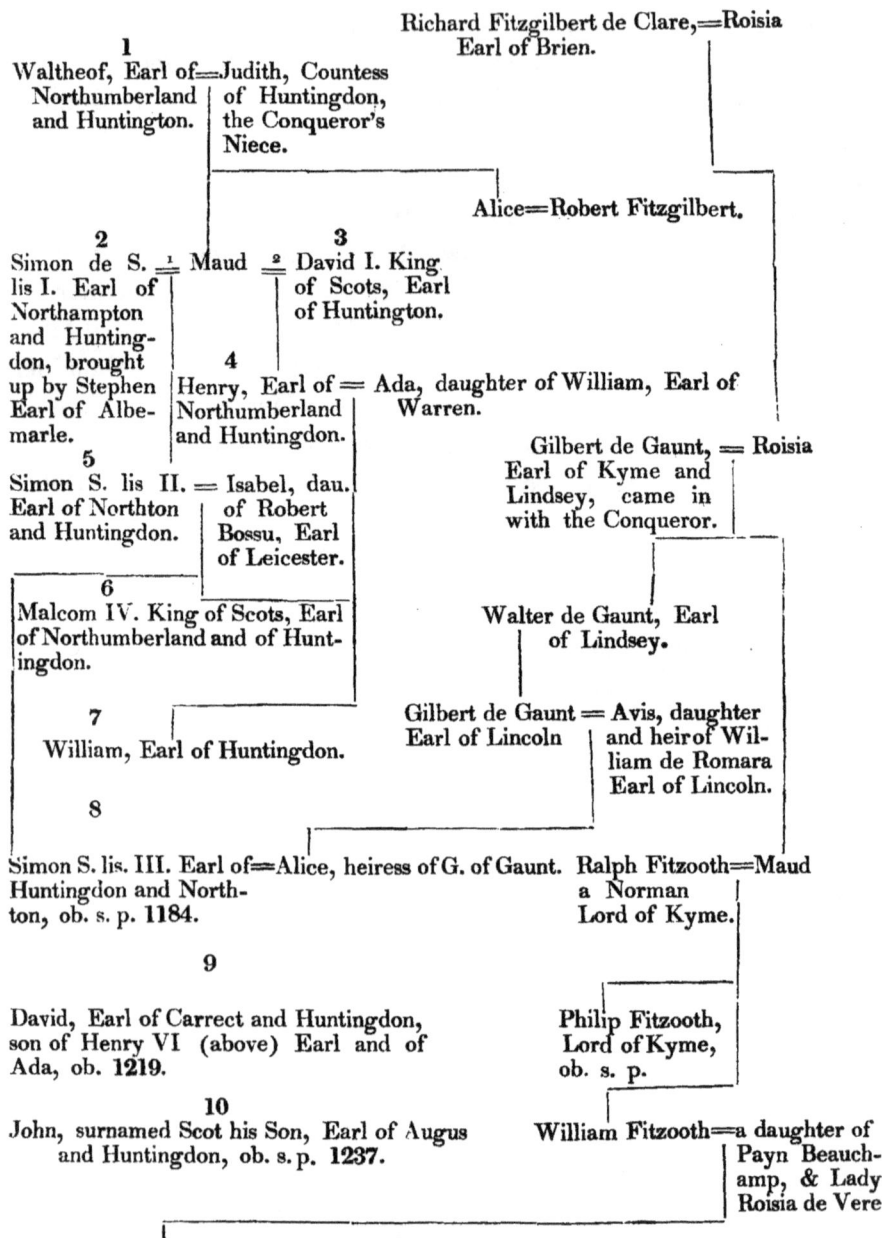

In the "Old Garland" it is said, that he was born at Loxley, in Staffordshire:* and in a shooting match made by the King and Queen, he was chosen by her Majesty as her archer † and she called him "Loxley;" a custom then common to style persons of eminence by the names of the towns where they were born.

If Robert Fitzooth, or his Father possessed any estate, it was doubtless seized on some political account, as it does not appear that any particular property was enjoyed by either.

In those days of Norman tyranny and feudal oppression, attainders and confiscations were frequent.

In the reign of Henry II, when Richard‡ the son of that king rebelled against his Father,—Robert de Ferrers manned his castles of Tutbury and Duffield in behalf of the Prince ǁ William Fitzooth, the Father of our hero, was connected with the Ferrers, and probably suffered with them in the consequences of that rebellion, which would not only have deprived the family of their estates, but also of their claim to the earldom of Huntingdon.

From some such cause, Robert Fitzooth was induced to take refuge in those woods and forests, where he had often found a safe and secure retreat, when fleeing from the demands of his country, or to avoid the ruthless hand of tyrannic power.

Tutbury, and other places in the vicinity of his native town, seem

* Or Loxley in *Nottinghamshire*. See " Ritson's Robin Hood."

† It is recorded, that on this occasion, Robin Hood was dressed in Scarlet, and his men in Green, "Lincoln Green," we presume according to "Ritson," and that they all wore black hats and white feathers.

‡ Afterwards Richard I, King of England :—he was seduced by the King of France. See J. P. Andrews Great Brit. and Europe, page 186.

ǁ See Hargrove's Anecdotes.

to have been the scenes of his "*juvenile frolics.*"* We afterwards find him at the head of two hundred strong resolute men, and expert Archers, ranging the woods and forests of Nottinghamshire, Yorkshire, and other parts of the north of England.

Charton, in his history of Whitby Abbey, records, that Robin Hood "when closely pursued by the civil or military power, found it necessary to leave his usual haunts, and retreating across the moors that surrounded Whitby, came to the Sea Coast, where he always had in readiness, some small fishing vessels; and in these putting off to sea, he looked upon himself quite secure, and held the whole power sent against him at defiance. The chief place of his resort at these times, and where his boats were generally laid up, was about six miles from Whitby, and is still called 'Robin Hood's Bay.'"

Several stratagems were used to apprehend this renowned person, but in vain. Force he often repelled by force, nor was he less artful than his enemies. At length, being closely pursued, after encountering many vicissitudes, and finding many of his followers slain, and the rest dispersed, he took refuge in the Priory of Kirklees about twelve miles from Leeds in Yorkshire, the Prioress being nearly related to him. According to Hargrove, " Old age, disappointment, and fatigue, brought on disease. A monk was called in to open a vein, who either through ignorance or design, performed the operation so ill, that the bleeding could not be stopped. Feeling that his dissolution was approaching, and desirous of pointing out the place where his remains should be deposited, he took his bow and discharged two arrows, the first fell in the river Calder,

* A phrase made use of by Dr. Fuller. See "Ritson's Robin Hood," page 16, in Notes and Illustrations.

the second falling in the Park, marked the spot for his future Sepulture."*

> "But give me my bent bow in my hand,
> And a broad arrow I'll let flee;
> And where this arrow is taken up,
> There shall my grave digg'd be."†

Robin Hood died on the 24th December, 1247, aged (about) 87. The following Epitaph was preserved by Dr. Gale, Dean of York, and inserted from his papers by Mr. Thoresby in his Ducat Leod and is as follows:

> HEAR UNDENEAD DIS LATIL STEAN
> LAIZ ROBERT EARL OF HUNTINDON,
> NEA ARCIR VER AZ HIE SA GEVD
> AN PIPL KAVLD IM ROBIN HEVD.
> SICK VTLAWZ AZ HI AN IZ MEN
> VIL ENGLAND NIVR SI AGEN
>
> Obit 24kal. Dekembris, 1247.

In a small grove part of the cemetery formerly belonging to this priory, is a large flat grave Stone, on which is carved, according to Hargrove, the figure of a cross of Calvary, extending the whole length of the stone, and round the margin is inscribed in monastic characters:

> DOVCE: IHV: DE: NAZARETH: DONNE:
> MERCY: ELIZABEH: DE. STANTON:
> PRIORES: DE: CETTE MAISON. ‡

* Admitting this interesting Anecdote to be true, we must conclude that Robin Hood shot his arrows, before his vein was opened.

† See Ritson's "Robin Hood," vol. 2. p. 186.

‡ This Norman Inscription shews its Antiquity—Robin Hood's Ancestors were Normans, and possessed the Lordship of Thyme in Lincolnshire. There is a Market Town in that County called Stanton.

The Lady whose memory is here recorded, is said to have been related to Robin Hood, and under whose protection he took refuge some time before his death. These being the only monuments remaining at the place, make it at least probable, that they have been preserved on account of the supposed affinity of the persons over whose remains they were erected.

In the church-yard of Hathersage, a village in Derbyshire, were deposited, as tradition informs us, the remains of John Little, the servant and favourite companion of Robin Hood.—" The Grave is distinguished by a large stone placed at the head, and another at the feet, on each of which are yet some remains of the letters I. L." (Hargrove)

Mr. Barrington remarks, "There is not on record, any particular cognizance of Military Archery from the days of Richard I; till the reign of Edward III, being an era of about a century and a half, when, as it appears, in the 15th year of his reign, that King issued orders for providing bows for the war against France:" and this writer says, "that the use of Archery, as expressly applied to the Cross or Long-bow, is not *mentioned* by our Chroniclers, *till* the death of Richard I, who was killed by a Cross-bow."*

A very little attention however to our best historical writers, will soon prove these statements of Mr. Barrington to be ridiculously erroneous!

Archers are mentioned in the accounts of the civil contests between Stephen and Matilda, and in the reign of Henry II.† according to Lord Littleton,‡ the English Infantry " consisted of Archers and

---
* See Roberts's English Bowman.
† In the 6th. year of this Monarch's reign, 1160, the renowned Robin Hood was born.
‡ See Lord Littleton, vol. 2. b. 2, p. 157.

Slingers," and we find this Prince frequently triumphing, by the power of his Archery!

We also read that at the battle of Cuton Moor, in Yorkshire, 22nd of August, 1138, between Stephen and David, King of Scotland, both armies had their archers, and that those of Stephen " Terribly galled the Galwegians," and obliged them to quit their post, after they had compelled his men at arms* to give way."

Giraldus† has justly celebrated the Welsh as most expert archers, and who vied with the English in their exploits with the Long-bow. The following feats of archery are related by this writer.

During a siege in Wales, " it happened that two soldiers running in haste towards a tower, situated at a little distance from them, were attacked with a number of arrows from the Welsh, which being shot with prodigious violence, some penetrated through the oak doors of a portal, although the breadth of four fingers in thickness The heads of these arrows were afterwards driven out and preserved, in order to continue the remembrance of such extraordinary force in shooting with the bow.‡

" It happened also in a battle at the time of William de Breusa, (as he himself relates,) that a Welshman having shot his arrow at a horse-soldier of his, who was clad in armour, and had his leather coat under it, the arrow, besides piercing the man through the hip, struck also through the saddle and mortally wounded the horse on which he sat."

* "Men at Arms" were Cavalry clad in armour; sometimes called by Froissart "Gens D'Armes," at other times "Lances" from the Spears or Lances they often carried. These soldiers fought both on horseback and on foot.

† "Giraldus Cambrensis" a cotemporary of Henry II.

‡ The bows of the Welsh, according to Giraldus, were made of Yew, and were of prodigious power.

"Another Welsh Soldier having shot an arrow at one of his horsemen, who was also covered with strong armour, the shaft penetrated through his hip, and fixed in his saddle:—but what is most remarkable, is, that as the horseman was in the act of turning round, he received another arrow in the other hip, which also passing through into the Saddle, firmly fixed the rider on both sides."

In the year 1298, Edward I. gained the great battle at Falkirk, over the Scots. Many thousands of the Scotch army, commanded by the Patriot Wallace, were left dead in the field.—This decisive victory was obtained chiefly by the power of the English archers.

Sir John Smith, in his discourse on Weapons, remarks on the exploits which were achieved by the archers under Richard I. in the Holy Land, " by overthrowing (principally by the wonderful effect of his archers) the brave Saladin and his whole army."

Mr. Gibbon notices the singular dread with which the English archers filled their enemies in the *Crusades*, and says, " that at one time, Richard, with seventeen knights and *three hundred archers*, sustained the charge of the *whole Turkish and Saracen army*." *

Speed records a feat of archery performed in the Holy Land, chiefly by means of an arrow.—" Certainly, he remarks, Hugo de Neville, one of Richard's special familiars, is recorded to have slain a Lion in the Holy Land, driving first an arrow into his breast, and then running him through with his sword."

The Scotch forces, under Archibald Douglas, in 1333† with most of the Scottish nobility, attacked the English at Halidown Hill, near Berwick.

* Cap 59—and quoted by Roberts;—who says; " It is to be observed that our historians seldom use the term *archer*, when they mean a Cross-bow-man."

† July 29th.—On this fatal day, about twenty thousand Scots were slain.

Edward III, here gained a most signal victory, in which his archers, as usual, had the greatest share. Douglas was slain, almost almost all his Nobles were taken or killed, and his Army was utterly destroyed, with hardly any loss on the side of Edward."*

A very few years after the above mentioned battle, at Halidown Hill, a great victory gave lustre to the arms of England, at sea.† "Four hundred stout ships with 40,000 men on board, were fitted out by Philip, to prevent Edward III from landing at Sluys. The English King had but 240 ships, but his own personal bravery, and the expertness of his seamen, carried the day; and 200 French vessels with 30,000 of their crews, afforded a glorious trophy of his success.

The extraordinary brilliancy of this victory, was attributed to the effect of the archers. Barnes says, speaking of the sea engagement before Sluys, "the English arrows fell so thick among the French, and did so sting, torment, and fright them, that many men, rather than endure them, leaped desperately into the sea."

A confirmation of this fact is recorded by Andrews.‡ "When the French courtiers did not venture to inform Philip of his defeat, a Buffoon undertook it! 'Cowardly, dastardly Englishmen,' cried he: 'how so?' said Philip. 'Because, they did not dare leap into the sea, as our brave men have done,' rejoined the Buffoon."

In the first part of this book it is stated, that the bow gained a hieroglyphical figure amongst the ancients, and was represented "as a king, and the arrow as an ambassador." Soon after the battle before Sluys, Philip of France refused a single combat with Edward of

* See Andrews's Great Britain and Europe. † Andrews's Great Britain and Europe.
‡ Andrews's Great Britain and Europe.

England. On this occasion, the following distich was written, and soon came into Edward's possession. The king was so pleased with it, that he swore "by St. George, that the verses were valiant verses," and he caused them to be shot from a Bow, into the town where the French king kept his residence:—

"Si valeas, venias Valois! depelle timorem!
Non lateas; pateas; moveas. Ostende vigorem."

IMITATED.

"Valois, be valiant! vile fear can't avail thee,
Hide not, avoid not, let not vigour fail thee!"

thus exemplifying the apparent prophetic allusion.

In the revolution which delivered the Swiss Cantons from the Germanic yoke, at the beginning of the fourteenth Century, the celebrated William Tell was the principal instrument. Grisler, the Austrian governor, exercised the most glaring acts of tyranny and oppression. Amongst others, he ordered his hat to be placed on the top of a pole, and commanded every one to pay the same respect to it in his absence, as to his person when present. Tell, refusing this base submission, was brought before the tyrant, who ordered him to shoot an apple from off the head of his son, the failure of which, was to have been the forfeit of his life. The boy was placed at 150 paces from his father. The latter drawing his bow with a trembling hand, let fly the arrow, and, fortunately, carried away the apple, amidst the shouts of thousands of spectators.

Grisler, perceiving that Tell had another arrow, partly concealed, asked him "for what purpose it was intended, as he was only to have had one shot?" to which he boldly replied, "To have shot thee, Tyrant, to the heart, if I had had the misfortune to kill my son."

So enraged was Grisler, that he ordered him to be bound, and carried prisoner to a place on the lake of Lucern. Tell however, escaped, and his fellow citizens, animated by his fortitude and patriotism, flew to arms, attacked and vanquished Grisler, who fell by an arrow from the hand of Tell. The consequence was, that the association for the Independency, took place on the instant.

The year 1346 will ever be remarkable in the annals of England. The "Great English Bow,"* now reigned in successive triumph over the foes of this Country, and our arrow seemed to be fulfilling its destiny, as the READY AND IRRESISTIBLE WINGED THUNDERBOLT OF THE LAND. Edward III, with a great inferiority of numbers, was attacked at Crecy, by the forces under Philip, consisting of at least 100,000 men, the Flower of the French forces. His well chosen position, his own coolness, and the steady valour of his men, aided by the despair of safety by any other means than their own exertions, gained him the most glorious victory which had ever yet been won. A strong body of Genoese cross-bow men, who marched in Philip's front, finding themselves much fatigued, had begged a short space to repose, and to dry the strings of their cross-bows. Philip refused this, and ordered them to advance. They marched forward, leaped thrice, and shouted at each leap, discharging their Cross-bows at the third, but ineffectually, for the shower that had fallen, had so wetted their strings, that each shaft fell short, while the arrows of the English, whose long bows had been covered with cases, each took effect.‡ This disheartened the Genoese, and when they fled, no pas-

* So called by Paulus Jovius, the celebrated Biographer of illustrious Men. See Roberts's English Bowman, page 14.
† See J. P. Andrews's, Great Britain and Europe.

‡ It is a singular fact, that most of our historians (following Mezeray, the French Chronicler) have remarked, that at this famous battle, the strings of the Genoese cross-bows were so much relaxed by rain, as to have been of little service. Some writers do not notice this disadvantage on the part of the cross-bow men, but only the superior effect of the English Long-bow. Muratori attributes the deficiency of the Genoese force, to the state of the ground, which was so soft, that when the cross-bow men attempted to put one foot in the stirrup of the cross-bow, in order to charge it, the other slipped from under them.

F

sage was allowed to the fugitives through the French ranks, that they might form in the rear of the army, but they were slain without mercy by the hands of Noblemen on Horseback, as enemies. The French Nobility having wearied themselves with slaughtering the runaways, rushed in confusion to attack the English.—They fell by hundreds under the English arrows.

Froissart, speaking of the battle of Crecy, says, "when the Genoese felt the arrows persyng thro' heeds, armes, and brestes; many of them cast downe their Cross-bowes, and dyd cutte their strynges and retourned discomfitted." The English Archers, according to custom stood in the form of an hearse about 200 in front, and 40 in depth,* when they were first charged by the infuriated French Nobles: and with this good order † "the wonderful effect of our archery and arrows was such, that flying in the air as thick as snow, with a terrible noise, much *like a tempestuous wind preceding a tempest*, they did leave no disarmed place, of horse or man, unstricken and not wounded."

It appears that the King of Bohemia, 11 other Princes, 80 Bannerets, 1,200 Knights, 1,500 of the Noblesse, 4,000 men at arms, and 30,000 private soldiers, all of the French army, were left on the field of battle; whereas, strange as it may appear, (and according to Andrews) three Knights, one Esquire, and a very few Soldiers, were all the loss on the English side.‡ And further, from Sir J.

* The ancient order of reducing archers into form, was into hearses, i. e. broad in front, and narrow in flank.
" These hearses of archers were placed either before the front of the armed footmen, or else in wings upon the corners of battalions, and sometimes both in front and wings." Sir J. Smith.

† See Sir John Smith.

‡ Stow relates the fact, that the English, under the Earls of Norwich, Salisbury, and Suffolk, "*with their wearied battailes*," joined the Prince after having supplied the exhausted Quivers of their archers with *arrows drawn from their dead and dying enemies.*"

Smith, we find "that the wonderful effect and terror of shot of arrows was on that day such, as neither the French King with his men at arms, nor any other of his great Captains with their brave and well armed bands of horsemen, of divers nations, were able to enter and break the archers, who with their vollies of arrows, did break both horsemen and footmen; wounding and killing both horses and men, in such sort, that the French King himself being in great peril, had his horse with the shot of arrows slain under him." Edward had not forces enough to take any other advantage of this wonderful victory, than that of besieging Calais; and it was before the walls of that place, that his ears were gladdened with the account of the battle fought between his troops, under the happy auspices of his Queen Philippa, and the Scots, who were utterly defeated, and their King, David Bruce, made a prisoner. At this famous battle of Durham, "Sir David Graham, a valiant Baron, with a wing of 500 horse, well appointed, gave a full charge upon the left flank of the English Archers, but was received with such a shower of arrows, that after two or three attempts in vain, having lost many of his men, he was fain to fly back to the main battle, upon the spur, in great danger of being taken.*"

Whilst Edward III, was engaged with his expedition which he made into Scotland, in 1355, his Son the Prince of Wales was playing the same part in France, with a chosen army, amounting to (at most) 12,000 men. He had carried destruction through Languedoc, and many of the finest provinces; when drawing near Poitiers, he found that King John, with 60,000 horse, and infantry in proportion, had so far surrounded his small force, that his retreat to Bourdeaux was cut off. Willing to save his gallant comrades from almost certain slaughter, he offered to give up his conquests, and

* Roberts.

not to fight against France for seven years. Nothing however, would be accepted, but his becoming a prisoner; the gallant youth replied, that "England should never have his ransom to pay."

On the morning early of September 19th, 1356, the battle of Poitiers began. The cool intrepid valour of the English, opposed to the impetuous, and ill regulated ardour of their enemies, exhibited precisely a second Crecy. At the first onset, the English Archers being judiciously posted in vineyards, and behind hedges, severally galled the assailants, who, consisting chiefly of dismounted cavalry, stumbled at every step, and became an easy mark for the hostile shafts. The slaughter was immense, and in a very short time, the defeat of the van-guard of the French, was completed. Those who took care of the Dauphin, frighted at the first appearance of a rout, left the battle that he might be safe; and the Duke of Orleans with three of the King's Sons and 800 Lances, accompanied their flight. Then the Lord Chandos crying aloud, "the Day is ours," the Prince of Wales attacked the main body of the French, and though King John and his youngest son, by their personal bravery during four hours, supported the dispirited legions, they were at length wearied out, and taken.

Sir John Smith relates, that at this great battle so glorious for the British Arms, "Prince Edward having not in his whole army above 8,000 English and Gascoins (of the which there were 6,000 archers, and 2,000 armed men) overthrew King John, (that valiant Prince,) who, at that battle, was accompanied with a great part of the nobility of France, and of other nations, as princes, dukes, earls, and other great captains, and had in his army above 60,000 horsemen and footmen, of the which there were above 10,000 men at arms, and of horsemen of all sorts above 30,000: where a little before the battle, the Prince, considering the small number that he had to make head and resist the French King with so huge an host, did take a ground of some strength and advantage for the guard of his flanks, and rear of his small army. Placing a great part of his archers in front, in the open place where the French horsemen and footmen were to enter, and give battle, the archers, with their wonderful vollies of arrows, did that day so wound, kill, and mischief both horses and men, that he overthrew King John of France with his whole army, and took him and one of his sons prisoners; and of earls, barons, knights, and esquires, to the number of 1,600, or more: besides that, there were slain, the Duke of Athens, with so many earls, barons, knights, and esquires, that they were numbered to be above 700, and so many prisoners of all sorts taken, that they far exceeded the number of the Prince's army."

Grafton says, "that at this battle of Poitiers, there were divers English Archers that had four, five, or six prisoners." Froissart particularly notices the regularity of the discharges of the English arrows, at this same battle, the effects of which he says were dreadful.

Not only large, but even very inconsiderable bodies of archers, have done great service in the field. Leland, in his "Collectanea" vol. 1, has mentioned several feats performed by a few English archers in France, in the time of Edward III,—Ascham, notices an action performed by Sir William Walgrave, and Sir George Somerset, with only sixteen English archers against a large body of the enemy, who were entirely routed by them. Barnes, among others, notices an action, which, in its effect, may well be ranked among the Wonders of Archery. This was the battle fought near Mauron, between Rennes and Plomerel, (15th August 1352,) between the English and French; the former, who were only 300 men at arms, and 600 archers, were led by Sir Walter Bentley and Sir Robert Knowles The army of the French and Bretons, being four times as great as that of the English, was under the conduct of Lord Guy de Nesle, Marshal of France, and other great officers; and was so ordered, that having a steep mountain behind at the back, the French and Bretons might be enforced to stand to it resolutely, by despairing to fly. This array was so dreadful, that it dismayed the hearts of several Englishmen, and they began to fly, and thirty of the archers actually deserted. But by the courage, good conduct, and resolution of Sir Walter Bentley, the English, after a doubtful and bloody fight, obtained a famous victory.

The battle of Naveretta in Spain, fought by the Prince of Wales in the reign of his Father Edward III, testifies "the wonderful effect of archers, where there were above 100,000 Spaniards, Frenchmen, Portuguese, Genoese, cross-bow men, and Moors, both horse-men and footmen, overthrown in that battle."

Walsingham, the historian gives a lively description of the effects produced by the bow, at the battle of Homildon hill, against the Scots, during the reign of Henry IV. in 1402, he says; "Thus the glory of the victory was entirely owing to the archers, who delivered their arrows, so briskly, so warmly, and so effectually, that they battered and bored the helmets, they split the swords, they shivered the lances, pierced through and through the men at arms, notwithstanding the armour with which they were clad, and even the best tempered mail, proved but a weak defence against the execution they did."— "The panoply worn by the Earl Douglas, who led the Scots in this battle, was of remarkable temper, * and that not only his armour, but that of his men at arms, had been three years in making, yet the English arrows rent it with little adoe;" and Douglas himself received five wounds.† Andrews writes, (speaking of this engagement)

* See Pinkerton's History of Scotland.

† Speed's Annals, p. 328.—It is recorded, that in this desperate conflict between the English and Scots, " the Men at Arms did not strike a stroke, or were not called much into action; they were little more than mere spectators of the valour and victory of the archers."

"Earl Douglas who led the Scots, enraged at the havoc made by the English archers, and trusting to the goodness of his armour, rushed forward, accompanied by eighty men of rank who were also clad in steel, to disperse that formidable corps, but was wounded in five places, and made a prisoner. Those eighty lords, knights, and gentlemen who accompanied the earl, soon had reason to repent their rashness, being "received by *showers* of arrows, which were discharged with so much force and effect, that no part of their armour could repel them."—These brave companions of Earl Douglas, were either killed or made prisoners with their leader.*

There is a recorded fact of a French soldier, who, in ridicule of the English archers, turned a little out of the ranks in an engagement between the two contending powers in Flanders, during the reign of Henry IV. (in 1402) and turning up his *bare-breech*, cried out, "*Shoote Englishe*," almost in the instant, an arrow from an English bow, was firmly fixed in the *Seat* of *Honor*, and before the Frenchman could recover himself from the unexpected blow, another shaft penetrated his body, and struck him to the earth.†

The battle of Shrewsbury which was fought in 1403, has been esteemed as one of the most desperate that England has ever seen. The archers on both sides, did terrible execution.—Henry IV. and the Prince of Wales on one side, and Earl Douglas with Henry, called Hotspur, son of the Earl of Northumberland, who agitated his rebellious movement,‡ on the other, performed prodigies of valour.

* Henry's History, vol. 5, page 463.

† This Anecdote appears to have been perpetuated by an engraving in Strutt's Horda Angel-Cynnan. See also Roberts's Eng. Bowman, p. 45.

‡ Northumberland not thinking his services properly rewarded, and disgusted at not having been permitted to ransom his Scottish Captives, amongst whom was the Earl Douglas, set them at liberty, and joined his forces to those of the Scots, against his Sovereign. See P. Andrews's Gt. Britain, &c.

At length, Hotspur being slain, and Douglas taken, Henry remained master of the field. Besides the vast slaughter amongst the private soldiers, not fewer than 2,291 gentlemen, on both sides, fell in this dreadful conflict, 200 of whom were natives of Cheshire.

Of all the actions that have been recorded, and handed down to us on the page of history, none are more highly calculated to create some touches of that respect and veneration for the long-bow, than the great and glorious Battle of Agincourt.

In the month of August 1415, Henry V left Southampton with an army of about 30,000 regular troops,—with which he besieged and took Harfleur, in six weeks after his landing on the coast of France.—An epidemic disease had greatly reduced the English forces, and Henry's army was also much lessened by a strong garrison left in Harfleur, and by many ships full of invalids who returned to England. The French had raised an army of at least 100,000 men, to oppose the invaders of their country.—The English army, after suffering in the manner just described, did not even according to the accounts of the French Historians, consist of more than from 20 to 25,000, but according to our best records, their numbers did not amount to more than 10,731 *on the eve of the battle.* Early on the morning of the 25th October, 1415, (the day appointed by the French, three days before the action,)* the English and French armies were ranged in order of battle, each in three lines, with bodies of cavalry on each wing. The Constable D'Albert† who commanded the French, fell in the snare that was laid for him, by drawing up his Army between two woods. This deprived him of the advantage he should have derived, from the prodigious superiority of numbers. His lines were formed unnecessarily deep, and his troops, particularly his cavalry, were so closely pressed together, that

---
* See J. P. Andrews's Gt. Britain and Europe, p. 20.—Henry V.
† In Andrews's History, the Constable's name is written "D'Albret."

they could hardly move or use their Arms. The first line of the French army consisting of about 80,000 men at arms on foot, with 4,000 archers, and 500 men at arms mounted on each wing, was commanded by the Constable D'Albert, the Dukes of Orleans, Bourbon and many other nobles. The second line was under the command of the Dukes of Alençon, Brabant, &c, and the third was directed by the Earls of Marche, Damartine, Fauconberg, &c. Henry employed various arts to supply his defect of numbers. He placed 200 of his best archers in ambush, in a low meadow, on the flank of the first line of the French. His own first line consisted wholly of Archers, four in file, each of whom, besides his bow and arrows, had a battle-axe, a sword, and a stake pointed with iron at both ends, which he fixed before him in the ground, the point inclining outwards, to protect him from cavalry. This was a new invention, and had a most happy effect. That he might not be encumbered, Henry dismissed his prisoners on their parole, to surrender themselves at Calais, if he obtained the victory, and lodged his baggage in the village of Agincourt in his rear. The command of the first line of the English army was, at his earnest request, committed to Edward, Duke of York, assisted by the Lords Beaumont, Willoughby and Fanhope. The second, was conducted by the King, with his youngest Brother, Humphry, Duke of Gloucester, the Earls of Oxford, Marshall, and Suffolk; and the third line was led by the Duke of Exeter, the King's Uncle. The lines being formed, the King in shining armour, with a crown of gold, adorned with precious stones on his helmet, and mounted on a fine white horse, rode along them. He addressed each corps with a cheerful countenance, and animating speeches, inflaming their resentment against the enemy, by telling them, that they had determined to cut off three fingers of the right hand of every prisoner, and he roused their love of honor by declaring, that every soldier in his army who behaved well, should thenceforth be deemed a gentleman and be entitled to wear coat-armour. When the two armies were drawn up in this manner, they stood a considerable time gazing at each other in solemn silence. The King dreading that the French would discover the danger of their situation, and decline a battle, commanded the charge to be sounded about 10 o'clock in the forenoon At that instant, the first line of the English, kneeled down, and kissed the ground, then starting up, discharged a flight of arrows, which did most dreadful execution amongst the crowded ranks of the Enemy.*

> "Upon the Horses as in chase they fly,
> Arrows so thick, in such abundance light,
> That their broad buttocks, men like butts might see,
> Whereat for pastime, bowmen shooting be."

The well directed, and repeated vollies of arrows from the first line, under the Duke of York, have been particularly compared to "the fall of a hail or snow storm." The confusion caused by the English archers among the enemy's horse was great, and almost instantaneous. The horses sides have been noticed as being "larded with Arrows." The archers being together in such great numbers, with their vollies of arrows, *"darken'd the air and dimm'd the light of the Sun"*† and while the French army rushed on the English with the frantic valour of an Indian intoxicated with opium, the gallant, but calm demeanor of Henry, which had inspired his soldiers with almost more than human courage, did, with the steady and suc-

* This first discharge of arrows, killed and wounded, *two thousand four hundred* men.

† See Sir John Smith's discourse on Weapons This expression respecting the appearance of arrows, is by no means hyperbolical. Historians of all ages have made similar obervations on their flights. So also many Poets.

> "————————And flang out such a flight,
> Of shafts, as well near seem'd t' eclipse the welcome light,
> And with the shots came shafts, like stormy showers of Hail."
> *Drayton.*

cessive discharges of arrows, effectually check the superficial torrent of the French fury. When the first line of the English, (with those in ambush) had expended their arrows, they advanced with swords and battle-axes, and completed the ruin of the opposing French cavalry.*

The first French line, was by these means defeated, and its leaders were either killed or taken prisoners. The second line commanded by the Duke D'Alençon, who had made a vow to kill, or take the King of England, or perish in the attempt, now advanced to the charge, and was encountered by the second line of the English conducted by the king. The conflict was more close and furious than the former, the Duke of Gloucester, wounded and unhorsed, was protected by his royal brother, till he was carried off the field. The Duke D'Alençon forced his way to the king, and assaulted him with great fury, but Henry brought him to the ground, where he was soon despatched. Discouraged by this disaster, the second line of the French army, made no more resistance, and the third fled, without striking a blow; yielding a complete and glorious victory to the English, after a violent struggle of three hours duration. The success of the fight, was greatly owing to our brave and irresistible archers, who galled the enemy with such "storms of arrows," that their multitudes at length gave way in every direction. Not fewer than 14,000 Prisoners were taken, a number that far exceeded the whole of the English Army.†

There is a muster-roll of the Army of Henry V, preserved amongst Rymer's unprinted collection in the British Museum. The Earl of

* The English Archers wore by their sides, battle-axes, small swords, and daggers. See Goodwin's History, Henry V, page 67.

† Besides the Dukes of Orleans, Brabant, Nevers, and Bourbon, the Marshall Boucicault, the Counts D'Eu Vindome, Richemont, and Harcourt, with 7,000 barons, knights, and gentlemen, were of the prisoners taken.

Cambridge appears in it, with a personal retinue, of 2 knights, 57 esquires, and 160 horse archers. The Duke of Clarence brought in his retinue, 1 earl, 2 bannerets, 14 knights, 222 esquires, and 720 horse archers. The roll includes 2536, men at arms, 4128 horse archers, 38 arblesters,* 120 miners, 25 master gunners, 50 servitor gunners, a stuffer of Bacinets,† 12 armourers, 3 kings of arms, a Mr. Nicholas Colnet, a physician, who brought 3 archers, 20 surgeons, an immense retinue of labourers, artisans, fletchers, bowyers, wheel-wrights, chaplains, and minstrels,—Foot archers are not enumerated, but the total number of effective soldiers, amounted to 10,731. THESE WERE THE MEN WHO GAINED THE FIELD AT AGINCOURT!

"In Henry VI. time," says Sir John Smith,‡ "John Lord Bellay, being accompanied with 200 Lances at the least, met by chance with an English Captain, called Berry, who had to the number of 80 archers; who perceiving the Frenchmen, presently reduced his men into an Hearse, turning their backs to a hedge, that the lances might only charge them in front; and so giving their vollies of arrows at the French lances charging, did so wound and kill men and horses, that they overthrew them, slew many, and took divers of them prisoners." "And within a while after," continues Sir J. Smith, "a French Captain, Guion de Coing, accompanied by 120 lances, went out to seek an adventure with the English, and was met by Sir William Olde, with 16 or 20 archers on horseback|| who dismounted, and formed in a broad way, where the lances could not charge them but in front: and the French charging them, the vollies of arrows of those few archers, wrought such notable

---

* "*Arbalister*" or Cross-bowman.

† A Stuffer of Bacinets,—one whose business it was to make and repair the padded lining of Helmets, &c. Bacinet is the light open helmet, generally worn at that period by the English Infantry.

‡ See Roberts's Eng. Bowman, 51. || Mounted archers were called *Hobulers*.

effect against the French horsemen, that they broke and overthrew them in such sort, that there were divers of the French slain, and many taken prisoners."

Sir John Smith also writes, speaking of the battle of Herrings, (so called by the French Chroniclers) fought in the reign of Henry VI. near Orleans, that this Engagement "doth evidently shew the great excellence of archery, against all other sorts of weapons; in which battle, Sir John Falstaff with other brave English Captains, by the Grace of God, and terrible shot of arrows, overthrew the Bastard of Orleans, the Lord High Constable of Scotland, the Count of Clermont, with many other Captains of great account, and their whole army of Frenchmen and Scots, in the which there were a great number of French harquebusseers and cross bow-men which against the archers wrought *no effect*."

The arrow seems to have been the decisive weapon at the great battle of Towton in Yorkshire, between the Yorkists and Lancastrians, during the reign of Edward IV. where 36,726 Englishmen, including almost all the surviving Nobility of England, who had escaped from former civil contests, fell a sacrifice to the ambition of contending Princes. The battle began about nine o'clock in the morning of the 29th March, 1461, the slain, according to Stowe were buried in five great pits in the field by North-Saxton Church. Amongst the killed, was Thomas Lord Clifford,[*] who met his death by a *headless* arrow piercing him in the throat, of which wound he immediately died.

The Nobility were so thinned in the civil war, particularly at this tremendous battle, at which, all in the kingdom were present, that

[*] This sanguinary Ruffian, (who was on the side of the Lancastrians) murdered the Infant Rutland, whom though but twelve years old, he slew in cool blood, in spite of the earnest prayers of a Priest his tutor.

in the ensuing parliament, only 1 duke, 4 earls, 1 viscount, and 29 barons, could be found to receive summonses, and attend the house. Henry VII instituted a band of archers to guard his person, under the title of "Yeoman of the Guard." This band was afterwards armed with swords and halberts, instead of bows.

In the year 1513, James IV. of Scotland invaded the English borders, while Henry VIII. was in France. The Earl of Surry, raised the militia of the northern counties amounting to 26,000 men, and advanced to meet him. The battle, which happened at Flowden field, was bloody, and terminated in the total defeat of the Scots with the loss of their king, the archbishop of St. Andrews, 2 abbots, 12 earls, and 17 lords. The victory in a great measure seems to have been owing to the archers under the command of Sir Edward Stanley. The van-guard of the English, was led by Lord Thomas, and Sir Edward Howard, the centre by their Father Lord Surry, and the rear, by Sir Edward Stanley: The Lord Dacres with a body of horse acted as a reserve. The King of Scots, exhorting his men to behave like soldiers, immediately sounded for battle. Sir Edward Howard for a long time sustained a heavy charge, and had nearly been routed by the singular valour of the Earls of Lenox and Argyle, but the Lord Dacres brought up the reserve, and restored the fight. Lord Thomas Howard met with brave resistance from the Earls of Crawford and Montrose. The King and Earl of Surry, maintained a long and sharp dispute until Sir E. Stanley brought up his archers who immediately let fly their arrows with such great force and effect, that the Scots were routed. The King perceiving the disorder, redoubled his efforts, and pressing forward with almost irresistible fury, would have overthrown the English Standard, but for the timely assistance of Lord Thomas Howard, who being joined by Lord Dacre's Horse, instantly gave a turn to the fortune of the day.—The Scottish Monarch with the flower of his Nobility, threw themselves into a ring, in which form they did all that men could do in defending themselves, nor did any one exceed the King in personal valour, but being mortally wounded in the forehead by an arrow, he fell, and with his life, ended this fierce and bloody conflict.

A Poem was written (as it is said) by one Henry Jenkins, a Schoolmaster, at Ingleton, in Yorkshire, to commemorate the great battle, and to record the names of the nobility and gentry who were present, with their tenants. It bears some interest, as it presents a striking picture of the manner of raising our ancient Militiamen, who were one day at the plough, and the next, ranged under the banners of their respective leaders, with arms in their hands, to use only against the hostile Invader, whom having repelled, the survivors returned to their homes and domestic employments This poem is a very long one, and as many of the names therein inserted, have long since past away, the following extracts from the production of the *poetical* Schoolmaster, are deemed sufficient in this work to shew the style of it. They afford some features of the historical facts of the great event which it was meant to record.

PART OF THE POEM OF "FLOWDEN FIELD."
BY HENRY JENKINS.*

Then might you see on every side,
The ways all filled with Men of War,
Here silken streamers waving wide,
There polish'd helms glist'ring afar.

* * * * *

* Henry Jenkins believed he might be about 12 years of age at the time of the battle of Flowden Field, when he was sent to Northalerton with a horse load of arrows, which a bigger boy had the charge of from thence to the army under the Earl of Surry.

Young wives did weep in woeful cheer,
To see their friends in harness drest;
Some rent their clothes, some tore their hair,
Some held their Babes unto their breast.

There woeful mothers mourning stood,
Viewing their Sons harnessed on horse,
And shouting shriek'd when they forth rode
And of their lives took little force.

From Penigent to Pendal Hill,
From Linton to Long Addingham,
And all the Craven coasts did till,
They wish the lusty Clifford came.*

All Staincliffe hundred went with him,
With striplings strong from Whoredale,
And all that Hanton hills did climb
With Longstroth elce and Littondale.

* * * * *

The right hand wing with all his route,
The lusty Lord Dacres did lead,
With him the bows of Kendal stout,
With milk coats and crosses red.

* * * * *

Thus Stanley stout the last of all
Of the rere-ward the rule did wield;
Which done, to Bolton in Glendale,
The total Army took the Field.

* Henry, the thirteenth Lord Clifford, on account of the hatred, the House of York, bore to his family, was concealed in the disguise of a shepherd, from seven years old, till he arrived at his thirty-second year, when in the first Parliament of Henry VII, he was restored to blood and honor, to all his Baronies, Lands, and Castles. He died **1523**.

Thus march'd forth these men of War,
And every band their banner shew'd,
And Trumpets hoarse were heard afar,
And glittering harness shining view'd,—

The sounding bows were soon up bent,
Some did their arrows sharp uptake;
Some did in hand their alberts hent,
Some rusty bills did ruffling shake.—

* * * * *

With the rereward the river past,
All ready in ranks and battle array,
They had no need more time to waste,
For victuals they had none that day.—

Yet they such stedfast faith did bear,
Unto their king and native land,
Each one the other did up cheer,
'Gainst foes to fight whilst they could stand.

And never flee whilst life did last,
But rather die by dint of sword;
Thus over plains and hills they pass'd,
Until they came to Sandiford.

A Brook of breadth a Tailor's yard,
Where th' Earl of Surry thus did say,
"Good fellow Soldiers, be not fear'd,
But fight it out like men this day."

Strike but three strokes with stomach stout,
And shoot each man sharp arrows three,
And you shall see without all doubt,
The beaten Scots begin to flee.

* * * * *

The Englishmen their feather'd flights
Sent out anon from sounding bow,
Which wounded many warlike Wights,
And many a groom to ground did throw.

* * * * *

Till at the last great Stanley stout,
Came marching up the mountain steep
His folks could hardly fast their feet,
But forc'd on hands and feet to creep.

"My Lancashire most lively Wights,
And chosen mates of Cheshire strong,
From sounding bow your feather'd flights,
Let fiercely fly your foes among."

The noise then made the mountains ring,
And Stanley, stout they all did cry,
Out went anon the grey goose wing,
And 'mongst the Scots did flickering fly.

The King himself was wounded sore,
An arrow fierce in's forehead light,
That hardly he could see his foes,
The blood so blemished his sight.

Yet like a Warrior stout he said,
And fiercely did exhort that tide,
His men to be no thing dismay'd,
But battle boldly there to bide.

But what avail'd his valour great,
Or bold device, all was but vain,
His Captains keen fail'd at his feet,
And Standard-bearer down was slain.

The Royal Corpse was found next morning, and conveyed to Sheene, a Monastery in Surrey, (where says Stowe) it "remained for a time, in what order I am not certain, but since the dissolution of the Abbeys in the reign of Henry VI, Henry Grey then Duke of Suffolk, keeping house there, shewed the same body, wrapped in lead and thrown into a waste room, amongst old timber, stone, lead, and other rubbish." A strange monument of human instability!

Amongst the various accounts which have been handed down to the present day, of the dreadful effects produced by the English Long-bow in battle, few perhaps can shew greater pretensions for record, than the following occurrence, which took place in the Isle of Wight in 1377, at about the commencement of the reign of Richard II.

The French invaded the Island, and landed in considerable force at "Franche-Ville,"* which town they burnt. After this, they marched in two grand divisions towards Carisbrooke Castle, for the purpose of taking that strong hold. One body filed off in the south east direction, the other kept the more northern road towards Newport. The news of this invasion, was soon spread throughout the Island, and no time was lost in collecting the forces which it possessed, to repel the foe. The English troops consisted principally of archers who were so admirably posted in ambush, that the French were easily decoyed to their own pending destruction. The enemy had gained the fields immediately under the west side of Noddies-hill, when the general attack and slaughter began. The crowded ranks of the French, who were now hemmed in a narrow road which led from Newport to Carisbrooke,† rendered their

* On the rebuilding of which it was called, and ever since has retained, the name of "Newtown."

† Since called "Dead-man's Lane."

downfall more ready and certain. Showers of arrows assailed them in such quick succession, that their resistance was but in vain. Each shaft seemed to be winged with certain death, for in a short time, the places ran with streams of blood. There was not one man left! About the same moment of time, the other body of the French attacked Carisbrooke Castle. The English, on completing the destruction of the enemy under Noddies-hill, lost not a moment in proceeding to the relief of the besieged, who, with the assistance of their brethren in arms, soon spread terror and dismay amongst the opening ranks of the French. Destruction quickly followed, and the woeful fate of the invaders was, in this additional instance, sealed by the ARCHERS OF ENGLAND..*

It appears that much attention was paid towards keeping the Forts and Castles of the Isle of Wight well supplied with arms. The following list is from an old record:—

A LIST OF BOWS AND ARROWS, &c. IN THE ISLE OF WIGHT, 1547.
"Remaining in the Forts in the Isle of Wight, 1547.

The Castell at Yarmouth

Bowes........140   Shriffs of Arrows......248
Bow Strings oone firkyne conteyninge 2 Grosse.

The Castell of Carysbroke

Chestes of arrows....59   Chestes of bowes....21
Bowstrings........3 Barrels.

The Castell of Sandham baye

Bowes....oone chest,   Sheiff Arrows....oone chest.

* This achievement, and other events glorious and honourable to the Islanders, have induced the present Society of Archers in the Isle of Wight, to call themselves "The Carisbrooke Archers."

The Castell at the Weste Cowe
in the Mayne Towne

Bowes........19   Chestes of Arrowes....32."

From Sir John Smith we read, that, in 1548, "Ambrose Earl of Warwick that accompanied the Duke of Northumberland his father, (then Earl of Warwick) a man of great valour, was sent by King Edward VI. as his Lieutenant-General, with an army of horsemen and footmen, to suppress the rebellion of Ket, in Norfolk, who at that time lay encamped with a great power of notorious and hardy rebels by the City of Norwich, upon a high hill called Mount Surrey. To the which city, the Duke with his army being come, he with gread order did encamp and lodge himself and his army on the other side of the city and river, and the next day entered the Town, and brought 24 field pieces to the chief charge, whereof he appointed Colonel Courpenick an Alman, and a great soldier, with his regiment of Almans, which was 1,200 strong, the most of them brave shot, and all old soldiers, with divers English bands, and valiant captains of our own nation, for the guard of the same: but before they could thoroughly entrench themselves, those furious rebels (contrary to all expectation) descended down their hill with such fury of shot of arrows, (being all bowmen, swords, and bills,) that they gave such a terror, and fear to our people, as they were fain to run away, with the loss of ordnance, and slaughter of a great sort of soldiers; and before the Duke could make head against them, they had taken 18 field pieces and carried them up to their hill, even with very force of men. And within two or three days after, those gallants did not let to abide the battle against the Duke and his whole army, in the plain field, where the battle was so manfully fought on both sides, that it would be hardly judged by the best soldiers that were there, which side was likely to prevail; but in the end (God giving the victory,) it was seen by that battle, that arrows were a most noble weapon. And whereas the Duke, who at his first assembling and forming his army changed many archers into harquebusseers, because he had no opinion of the long bow, he after the victory and suppression of the rebels upon the experience that he had of the *danger* and *terror* of *arrows*, his own horse being wounded under him at that battle, with three or four arrows whereof he died, did, both then, and many times after, openly protest his error, before Count Malatesta Baglion, an ancient and noble soldier, and other great Captains, saying, that from that time forward, he would hold the *bow* to be the *only weapon of the world*. And this I have set down almost *verbatim*, from the report of the aforesaid Ambrose Earl of Warwick, who was present at that action, and had his horse wounded under him with two or three arrows."

Also about the year 1562, during an engagement between the English and French and Alman companies, near Newhaven, in which the enemy were greatly superior in number and "forced the English to retire, it happened," says Sir John Smith, "that eighty tall archers, (Hampshire Men) did at that time land in the haven, who taking their bows and sheafs of arrows, with their other furniture, did presently march without any tarryance through the town into the field where the skirmish was; upon whose coming, the English bands that a little before were forced by the often charges, and great multitude of the shot of their enemies, to retire even to the very town ditches and gates; taking courage afresh, they and the bowmen entered again into skirmish with the Almans and French; the *eighty archers* did behave themselves so notably against the enemy, with their vollies of arrows; that with the brave and valiant charges which they and the rest of the English bands gave upon their enemies, (but chiefly with the *excellence of the archers,)* they forced them to turn their backs and routed them, and became masters of the field. Upon which notable effect, of those few archers, as also upon divers others that Colonel Alman, the Reingrave, had before time seen in serving against the English, he shortly after, upon the return of a message sent by the Earl of Warwick, (Sir Edward Horsey being the Messenger,) did most highly commend the notable effects, that he long before, in divers services, had seen performed by English *archers*, both against horse and foot; and said also, that long before that time, he knew by experience that great numbers of English archers were able to perform great matters in the field: but that so small a number of bowmen, as were in that last great conflict, should be able, with their arrows to do so great mischief against his old bands of Almans, French, and Gascoignes, he could not have believed, if he himself had not seen it. And therefore he did with great reason and experience protest and acknowledge, the long-bows of England to be the most excellent weapons for the field, that were used by any nation in Christendom."

Further, Sir John Smith relates " in our time, King Henry VIII. being at the siege of Teroüenne, a convoy with provisions was coming from Guienes, towards Teroüenne: the French Captains of Picardy, and Vermandois having intelligence of it, assembled all the men at arms, harquebusseers, and Cross-bow men, laid in ambush, and overthrew the English light horse Avan-couriers; which being perceived by the English, they so placed their archers, that after a long fight, and many charges by the French men at arms, and their shot given, (the French far exceeding the English in number) the French having a number of horses wounded and slain, were completely repulsed, and overthrown by the *excellence of the archers.*

From Neade, we fine that Henry VIII. won Turwin, Tournay, and Boulogne, chiefly by the use of the bow, which " amazed the enemy, and wounded almost every one." Such was the effect of well directed vollies of arrows.*

Henry VIII. was an Archer.

In the reign of Elizabeth we learn, that the bow was extolled, and its value in military service, highly spoken of, not only by Englishmen, but by foreigners of high rank, and great military skill, who had witnessed its powerful effects. During this Queen's reign, 50 bowmen were on board each of the first rate Men of War, and the inferior rates also had a due proportion of archers, and, according to Sir J. Smith, a considerable part of the army drawn out at Tilbury, to oppose the Spanish Invasion, anno. 1588, consisted of Bow-men.

In 1643, the Earl of Essex issued a precept, "for stirring up well affected people by benevolence towards raising a company of archers for the service of King Charles I. and the Parliament.—And in the pamphlet (noticed by Grose) printed 1664, giving an account of the success of the Marquis of Montrose against the Scots, bowmen, are repeatedly mentioned. This, it appears, is the latest period to which any account of English military archery can be traced,† or that the bow has been held in requisition as an implement of war.

"Thou yieldest to Fate,
"Thy pride is fall'n, thy ancient Glories end."

The records from which the foregoing anecdotes are selected, show that with the power of the English archers, has France been ten times successfully invaded,‡ once brought to the brink of ruin under Edward III. once conquered by Henry V. one of her monarchs, viz. King John at the battle of Poitiers, with his son Philip and most of the French nobility made prisoners, and Lewis

* Lord Herbert tells us that of the ten thousand Men sent against France, 2,000 were archers.—

† See Roberts's English bowman. p. 65.

‡ In 1339, 1346, 1355, 1359, 1415, 1417, 1421, 1475, 1513, 1544.

An Ancient Archer,
with his Sword and Leaden Maul.
and Bow and Arrows.

XI. of France, submitted to pay a tribute to Edward IV. to relieve himself from the terror of the English arms.

> " Thus thou peculiar Engine of our Land!
> Weapon of conquest! Master of the Field!
> Renowned Bow! (that mads't this Crown command,
> The Tow'rs of France, and all their pow'rs to yield,)
>
> * * * * *
>
> Thou first didst conquer us; then raised our skill,
> To vanquish others:—
> And now, how com'st thou to be out of date,
> And all neglected leav'st us, and art gone!
> And with Thee th'ancient strength, the manly state,
> Of Valour and of Worth, that Glory won?
> Or else stay'st thou 'till new priz'd shot abate,
> (That never shall effect what thou hast done)
> And only but attend'st some blessed reign,
> When thou and Virtue shall be grac'd again.*

OF THE DRESS OF AN ANCIENT ENGLISH ARCHER,
(ACCORDING TO GROSSE,)
WITH REMARKS ON HIS EQUIPMENT AND EXERCISE.

The Dress of our ancient archers, is given (Grosse remarks, in his Antiquities) in several chronicles. Fabian says "The yeomen hadde, at those dayes, their lymmes at libertye, for their hoseyn were then fastened with one point, and their jackes were longe, and easy to shote in, so that they mighte drawe bowes of great strength, and shote arrowes of a yarde longe. Captains and officers should be

* Daniel's History of the Civil Wars.

skillfull of that most noble weapon, and to see that their soldiers, according to their draught and strength, have good bowes, well nocked, well strynged, everie strynge whippe in their nocke, and in the middes rubbed with wax, braser and shuting glove, some spare strynges trymmed as aforesaid, everie man, one sheafe of arrows, with a case of leather defensible against the rayne, and in the same shefe, (or 24 arrows) whereof eight should be lighter than the residue, to gall and astoyne the enemye with the hail shot of light arrowes, before they shall come within the danger of their harquebuss shot. Let everie man have a brigantine or a little cote of plate, a skull, or huffkyn, a maule of leade of five foot in length,* and a pike, and the same hanging by his girdle, with a hooke, and a dagger. Being thus furnished, teach them by musters to march, shoote and retire, keepinge their faces upon the enemy. Sumtyme put them into great nowmbers, as to battell apperteyneth, and thus use them oftentimes practised, till they be perfecte, for those men in battell, ne skirmish cannot be spared. None other weapon may compare with the same noble weapon."

OBSERVATIONS ON THE UTILITY OF THE BOW,

AS A WEAPON OF WAR.

On entering into the examination of the merits of our ancient weapons, which once gave us with inferior numbers, so decided a superiority over our enemies, it may be remarked, that, on a com-

* This maule was for the purpose of despatching the wounded, (most probably those only who were *mortally* wounded.) These instruments of *butchery*, were used as late as the time of Louis XII. who died in 1524.

parison with the effect of small arms, the total disuse of the Long-bow, in the field, has been directed without due consideration, and that in the decision, as has been observed by Mason and others, blind prejudice prevailed over experience.*

"The Bow is evidently the only weapon, that can always afford advantage, (even to great inferiority of numbers) from its excellence depending on greater powers of strength, activity, and calm resolution, for which the English soldier has ever been justly remarked, over all the other troops of the earth."

Mr. Mason clearly shews, that the Long-bow is the only efficient weapon *of reach*, that can conveniently be used with the pike, without being cumbersome, and he proves, that were the use of the Long-bow *added to our present mode of warfare, much advantage would be gained!*

It appears from a statement by Marshall Count Saxe, in his memoirs, that on a computation of the balls used in a day's action, not one of upwards of eighty-five takes effect: and Mason remarks, "By the observation on battles of a later date, the effect falls infinitely short of the above proportion; which can be clearly proved by the review of the various actions of the present day." He cites the effect of musketry, at the battle before Tournay, May 22nd, 1794, between the French and the Allies, from six o'clock, A.M. till nine at night. The French lost, at the highest calculation, 10,000 men, killed and wounded; and the Allies 5,000. The ground was open. The French brought into action 100,000 men, the Allies 60,000. Reckoning the proportion of our infantry, at 40,000, and supposing

* See Mason's "Considerations of the reasons that exist for reviving the use of the Long-bow, with the Pike." Published by Egerton, Whitehall, 1798.

N.B.—This excellent little work, might prove a complete "*Drill Sergeant*" to a corps of archers!

at a moderate average, that each man expended 32 rounds, a total of 1,280,000 balls were discharged, to occasion the above loss of the enemy, making 180 shots to the disabling of one object, without bringing into computation the proportion of the loss, that might have been occasioned by the bayonet, the cavalry, and artillery, though these causes on that day, may reasonably be concluded to have occasioned half the loss. In this case, upwards of 236 shots of musketry must have been fired, to have disabled one man. The effect of a musket ball cannot be judged of, according to its great extent of range, if shot in elevation, which may be about 1,000 yards. It cannot be exactly determined, but by its efficient direction within a reasonable distance; which, as the place is levelled, is reduced, at the highest elevation to about 200 yards, and the aim at this distance is very uncertain. The common range of an ancient English-long-bow, when discharged in elevation, was from 9 to 12 (and 15*) score yards, and sometimes more. From the greater pressure of air on the shaft, than on the bullet, and from the gravity being in the pile, it would descend at its ultimate distance, before it had lost its force, and would then do execution, whereas, the force of ball in a like situation, would be spent.

A bullet, if it miss its direction, by overshooting the object, will most probably go to its utmost range without effect; whereas, the arrow, if it miss the front rank, may yet descend on the rear, and do equal execution; at least, one shaft in ten would strike. Here then evidently appears an advantage in favour of the bow, in point of certainty of shot, of no less than upwards of twenty to one! and as an archer can discharge at least two arrows for one musket shot, even this proportion is doubled.

* The English archers would frequently discharge their flights of arrows at the enemy, at fifteen and sixteen score yards distance, particularly at the approach of large bodies of horse or on the enemy's infantry coming down in close columns.

In the foregoing well authenticated anecdotes, it has been shewn, that the ancient English archer could pierce the stoutest and best tempered steel armour, such as had required three years for its completion, and the most careful management in the course of its manufacture. The present Austrian cuirassier, carries a breast plate made musket proof. Now, as we may presume that a soldier of the nineteenth century, cannot bear more weight of armour, either partially or generally,* than one of the days of Edward III. could, it may be concluded, that the force of the arrow must have been more effective, than the modern bullet *from the common musket*. In these days, however "of noise and smoke," imagination alone is left to enable us to form conjectures of the prodigious power and terrific effect of the ancient English Long-bow and arrow, as a weapon of war. We may say, that scarce a shadow remains of that substance, which once was so truly formidable to our enemies.

Mason supposes a body of 1000 archers opposed to another body, not archers, of even great superiority of numbers, "What impression," he remarks, "must it not have on the enemy, the sight, and effect of at least 6000 arrows flying on their line in a minute! Under such flights kept up without intermission, how would it be possible for either horse or foot, to perform their evolutions, or not fall into rout and disorder, amidst such carnage, and *visible* danger? Musketeers, are enabled to keep their order, as opposed to each other from not seeing the missiles sent against them."

Sir John Smith, in his discourse on weapons, says, "Bullets discharged are invisible, therefore do no ways terrify the sight; and by reason of their frequent failing in their points and blanks, do then

---

* A whole suit of armour is more easily worn, then a heavy breast plate alone, as the weight of the former is equalized. A girl carrying a single pail of water, performs her office with more fatigue, than if she carried the like weight in each hand.

neither kill nor hurt. Howbeit, the vollies of arrows, flying together in the air, as thick as hail, do not only terrify, and amaze in most terrible sort, the ears, eyes, and hearts, both of horses and men, with the noise, and sight of their coming, (much like a tempestuous wind, preceding a tempest,) but they also in their descents, do not leave in a whole squadron, so much as one man unstricken, and not wounded with divers arrows, if the number of the archers be answerable to the number of the squadron. And therefore, for the experience that both I, and many others, both noblemen, gentlemen, and great captains of many nations that I have served amongst, have had of the small effect of weapons of fire in the field, with the reasons and differences before alledged;—for my part, I will never doubt to adventure my life, or many lives, (if I had them,) amongst *eight thousand archers*, complete, well chosen, and appointed, and therewithal provided and furnished with great store of sheaves of arrows, as also with a good overplus of bows and bowstrings, against *twenty thousand* of the best *harquebussiers and musqueteers*, that are in Christendom."*

Sir John Smith, speaking of such "men of war," as seemed to prefer the musket to the bow, says, "by which their opinions and reports, it seemeth, that as they are utterly ignorant and without any experience of the effects of archers, so are they as ignorant of all notable histories; or else, according to the new fashion, they do believe nothing but that which they themselves have seen, which in troth appeareth to be very little." The pen of Sir John Smith, has furnished us with many interesting anecdotes and reflections on the value of archery. His opinions on the long-bow, as a weapon of

* Had Sir John Smith, who was so great a soldier, and who had gathered so much experience in warfare which fell to his lot, lived to have witnessed the perfection to which the *rifle* has been brought, he would not probably have classed or included *such* an instrument with the common musquet of the time of Henry VIII.

war, were looked upon with much respect; he was a warm advocate for the continuation of the use of it in the field, with the fire arms of the day, and so were also many other great officers of experience.

Clement Edmunds* writes, "The disorder or routing of an enemy which is caused by the bowmen, cometh from the fearful spectacle of a drift of arrows: for a shower of arrows well delivered and well seconded, for a while is so terrible to the eye, and so dreadful in success, that it is almost impossible to keep the enemy from routing: for, whereas the cloud of arrows is subject to the sight, and every arrow, is both suspected and able to bring death sitting on the head, an enemy is as much troubled at such arrows as come fair upon him and do not hit, as those that do hit; for no man is willing to expose his flesh to open and imminent danger, when it lieth in his power to avoid it, and therefore, while every man seeketh to avoid hurt, they fall into such confusion, as besides the loss of particular men, the enemy can hardly escape disorder, which is the greatest disadvantage that can befall him. The barbed heads of arrows are not easily pulled out, which maketh the soldiers not mind the fight, untill they be delivered of them, and the horse to fling and chafe, that it is impossible they should either keep their rank, or be otherwise managed for any service."

It has been observed, that the point blank range of a musket shot, is about 120 yards, but that in action, it cannot be much depended on beyond 100. Beyond 80 toises or 160 yards, the fire of a line of infantry can seldom have a *great* effect.‡ The descent of a flight of arrows at nearly double this distance, suppose upon a column of

* Clement Edmunds, wrote about the close of the 17th century.

† Sir John Haywood remarks, that the eye in all battles, is first overcome.

‡ Gilbert, Vol. 1, page 157—See Instructions for the drill, as ordered for his Majesty's Forces. By J. Russell, Brevet Captain, &c. 2nd edition, 1799.

cavalry, or upon a column of infantry, is as certain for killing, wounding, and throwing into disorder, as at 160 yards. Also, the strong steel pointed head of the arrow would, in some respects, give it the advantage of the leaden bullet.

Experiments have lately been made, to ascertain the claim for certainty of shot, between the musket and the bow. In order to accomplish this design, one of the best muskets was loaded with the greatest nicety, the powder used, was of the best quality, and the quantity was previously weighed, and proportioned with the utmost exactness to the weight of the ball, which was confined with muslin or fine rag, instead of paper. In short, every precaution was taken, to afford the musket its true and full effect. The victory was to be decided in twenty-one shots at a small target, distance 100 yards, and the result of the trial was, that out of twenty-one shots, the musket put eleven, and the bow fifteen, into the target. The experiment was repeated *twice*, but the bow continued the successful weapon.* This trial, however, could not shew the advantage of the bow over the musket, in its fullest point of view; for had an army been shot at, instead of a target, every arrow which went wide of or *over* the mark, would have taken place, while the bullet, having passed over the heads of the front rank, would probably pass over the heads of the other ranks.

A variety of positions might very readily be shewn, wherein the bow could prove itself to be a most effective weapon, even in modern warfare.† The bow and musket should they ever be brought

* Roberts's English Bow-man, page 71.

† Arrows charged with fire, and adhering to men and horses, (which, by a pamphlet in the British Museum, called, "A New Invention for shooting Fire Shafts in the Long-Bow, 1698," appears to have been the case in former times,) may readily be conceived to be productive of immediate disorder, amongst the Enemy. The service also of barbed arrows charged with fire, is in firing combustible places, also the enemy's tents, sails of ships, &c. and in molesting the cannoniers, particularly by night, the archers having of course previously ascertained the distances, all which is peculiarly adapted for the service of Archery in general.

together in the field, might, with good regulations, be made materially to assist and to support each other. The arrow might frequently be called into action, to the check and annoyance of an enemy, when the musket would be wholly useless; and in many cases, in conjunction with musketry, where great unevenness of ground existed, &c. If these weapons should ever be found in aid of each other's powers, then the wonder will be more generally excited, that the bow had been so long neglected.

PART II.

ARCHERY VALUABLE AS AN AMUSEMENT.

If in the advancement of Arts, the "terrific bow and war-sheaf" be now laid aside, and doomed to give place to the "noisy and smoaky firelock," the neglected implements may still claim the protection of the wealthy, as capable of affording much recreative pleasure, in one of the most elegant, the most interesting, and at the same time one of the most healthful amusements known. The terrors of the bow have now vanished. That weapon by which nations subverted nations, "the bow of remote antiquity,[*] once so destructive, so bloody, so cruel, is now known only as an instrument of polite amusement; and a company of archers, at this day, appears less hostile, than the gladiators of a fencing-school." In this country, in particular, the bow has been stamped with honours sufficient for the establishment of its everlasting fame.

Archery is an honourable pastime. As we become more acquainted with the art, it more forcibly draws forth the natural tribute of gratitude for past services, and insures for itself a never fading interest, and attachment. It is an exercise adapted to every age, and to every degree of strength, and is not necessarily laborious; and perhaps there is no amusement that more awakens and enlivens

[*] See Mosely on Archery.

the active powers, and creates so little satiety. In the practice of it, not only does the archer walk over much more ground, than on ordinary occasions of pleasure he would voluntarily do,* but, by shooting, his arms become nervous, and his muscular powers increase to a degree, not readily to be conceived. Besides the temporary gratification to be derived from shooting, and the fact of its being calculated to promote every pleasure, to be derived from the most agreeable society, the art of archery holds out the strongest inducement on the score of health, to value and to use it as an exercise. There is a remarkable instance recorded of the efficacy of shooting in the Long-bow in restoring health, in the case of the father of the present Mr. Waring, of Caroline Street, Bedford Square, London. Mr. Waring had contracted an oppression in his chest; but by the practice of shooting whilst he was staying at Sir Ashton Levers, he recovered greatly. So evident did it appear, that this exercise had greatly benefited Mr. Waring's health, that Sir Ashton was induced to take it up, and his example was followed by many of his friends, who in the year 1780, formed themselves into a society under the title of "Toxophilites." This Society of Archers was the parent stock of numerous others known at this day.

There are few diversions in the open air, in which Women can join with satisfaction, Archery, however, is one of those few. In the pursuit of this elegant art, it was long since sufficiently proved, that it is perfectly adapted for female recreation. The opinion that the practice of it is too masculine for Ladies is quite erroneous: †—This

* In walking fifty times from target to target, distant 100 yards, an archer goes over a space of ground nearly equal to three Miles.

† The practice of archery appears to be rapidly increasing, and there is hardly a county in England without one archery society or more than one belonging to it: and in which are generally to be found Ladies of the first rank and fashion, whose appearance on the target grounds renders the same at all times particularly lively, and interesting.

censure, which has been attempted to be cast upon it, is unmerited and illtimed.—We find on record, that Margaret, daughter of Henry VII. killed a buck with an arrow, in Alnwick Park, in Northumberland, in a hunting party. Queen Elizabeth, while on a visit at Lord Montecute's, at Cowdry in Sussex, slew three deer with her bow and arrows. Indeed, archery has always been esteemed as a fit and elegant amusement for Ladies. In the meetings for shooting, all are elevated with the same object of emulation. A high degree of sparkling interest is kindled in a moment in every breast. Each grace possessed by the individual, is displayed in the various proper attitudes, which archery requires, viz: in standing, nocking, gently raising the bow to its proper pitch, drawing up the arrow and loosing it to the mark. The attitude of an archer drawing the bow, has been deemed worthy of notice, and cannot fail to display, in a considerable degree, the graces of the female form. And let it be observed that the address of an archer or archeress, while at the exercise of shooting in the open air in the field, may be as attractive to the eyes of the beholder, as the display of a dance in the confined atmosphere of a ball room. This remark may create a smile on the cheek of the Fair, who may not yet have experienced the pleasures of archery. Each recreation, however, has its own particular moment for enjoyment, and perhaps it may be fairly said, that the one is greatly calculated to enchance the pleasures of the other. "The bow, in the hands of the British fair, presents a new era in archery." To its ancient honors it has added novel and unexpected graces, and tends to assimilate itself with the arts of peace, and forms a new link in the chain of society.

"The appearance of an arrow on the wing," says Mosely, "viewed on one side, is singularly interesting." Its steady movement, the curve it describes, its ascending and descending motion, and its velocity, are beauties which never fail to excite agreeable feelings in the mind, and even lead us for a moment to attribute active powers, to the shaft. Weakness and strength are well expressed by the arrow which arrives short, or which passes far over the target; and the different degrees of swiftness perceptible in arrows from bows of various powers, immediately associate the ideas of bodily vigour in various degrees of strength.

Ascham strongly recommends the practise of archery, as tending " to invigorate the nerves, and to increase the strength of the body." " That the labour which is in shooting, of all other is best, not only because it increaseth strength, and preserveth health most, but because it is not vehement, but *moderate*, not over-layinge one parte with wearinesse, but softly exercisinge everye parte with equalnesse; as the armes and breastes with drawinge, the other partes with goinge, being not so painful for the laboure, as pleasure for the pastime, which exercise (by the judgement of Physitions) is most alowable;" and, as Roberts remarks, " We see old archers, continue the diversion with satisfaction to themselves, and pleasure to others, and although when far advanced in life, they find their strength somewhat give way, yet do they not perceive any loss of *skill* in the art. By changing their strong bows for others which are weaker, they seldom perceive the want of very powerful nerves; but, in pursuing this amusement, can " bid old age grow green, and wear a second spring." Sir William Wood, who, it must be hoped, was a better archer than poet, in his " Bowman's Glory," writes:

> "It is an exercise (by proof) we see
> Whose practice doth with nature best agree,
> Obstructions of the liver it prevents,
> Stretching the nerves and arteries, gives extent
> To the spleen's oppilations, clears the breast
> And spungy lungs; it is a foe profest
> To all consumptions."

Dr. Mulcaster, a contemporary of Ascham, has said, speaking of archery, "To say enough of this exercise in few words, which no words can praise enough for the commodities which it bringeth to the health of the body, it consisteth of the *best* exercises, and the best *effects* of the best exercises."

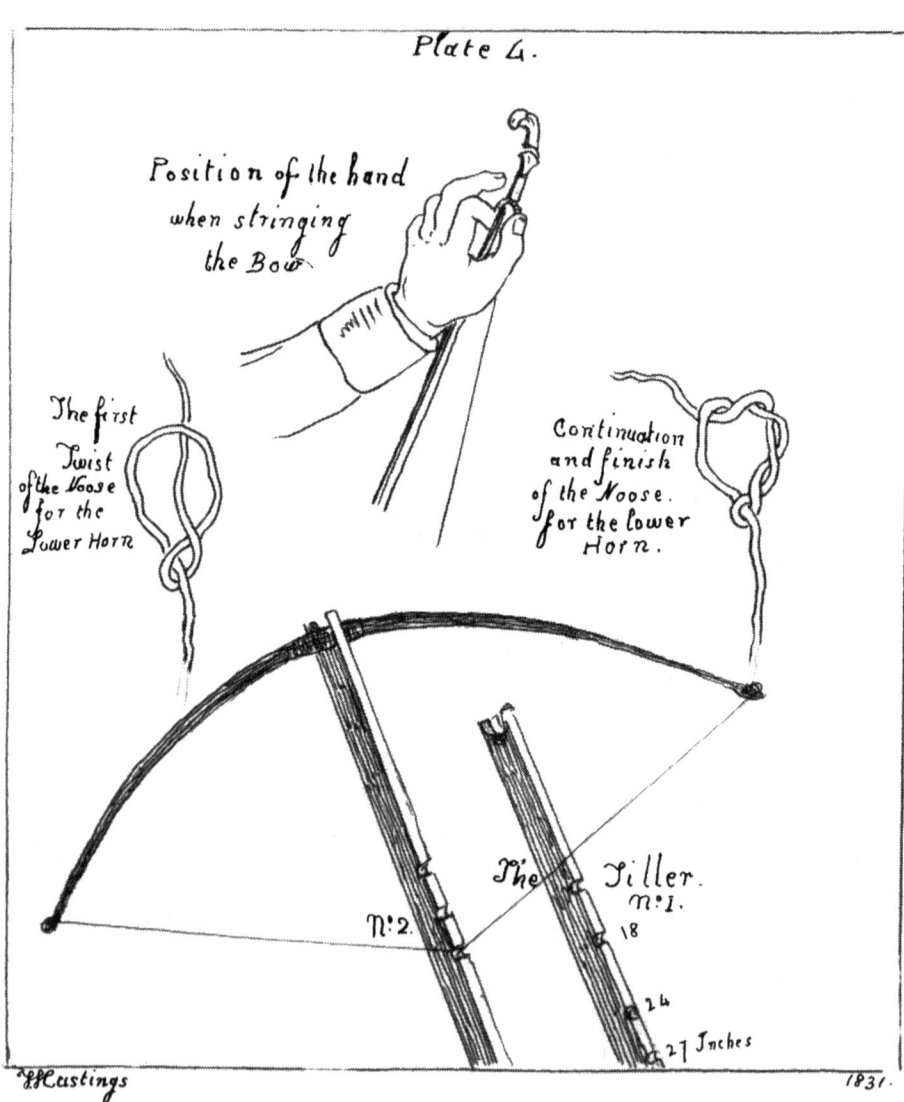

PART III.

THE ART AND PRACTICE OF ARCHERY.

All arts are more properly the subjects of imitation than of description, particularly in respect to manual operation, and corporal attitudes.

Since the days of Ascham, archers have looked up to him as their polar-star, for almost all matter relating to their art. Ascham, however, seems to have found a difficulty in conveying a clear and satisfactory explanation of those minutiæ, necessary for the perfection of an archer. He observes, speaking of the nicety of action, "that it is more *pleasant to behold, than easy to be taught; not so difficult to be followed in practice, as to be described.*" And speaking of shooting well, he says, "I can teach you to shoote faire, even as Socrates taught a man, once to know God; for when he asked him what was God, nay, sayth he, I can tell you better what God is not!—God is not evil, &c. &c. This sort of *reversed* instruction, for *some* points of the matter under contemplation, may be better than the ordinary mode of teaching, and many little niceties necessary for the archers' attention, may sooner be understood by this method.

The bow appears to be so simple an instrument, that one might be apt to imagine, it does not require any study; yet without a theoretical knowledge of it, the practical part can never be properly attained. The first thing necessary for the young archers' attention, is, to recollect that the flat part of the bow is the back, and the round part, the belly, which is always to be bent inwards.* An attempt made to bend a bow the reverse way, will cause it to fly instantly.

ON STRINGING.

In stringing, the handle of the bow, which is the centre of action should be firmly grasped with the right hand, taking care that the string be not twisted, and that the back, or flat part, be towards the body, and the wrist of the right hand close against the side or hip. The lower limb of the bow, which has always the shortest horn, is to be placed on the ground, against the inside of the right foot, to prevent the bow from slipping. Let the left leg be about three quarters of a yard apart from the right, and rather forward, and the knee kept quite straight. The right knee may be bent at convenience. Having thus secured a firm position with the bow, put that part of the left hand, which is close to the wrist, on the upper limb of the bow, letting the thumb lightly embrace the outer part, and the forefinger, i.e. about the first joint, the inner part of the eye of the string. Then pull the bow up sharply with the right hand, and at the same time, press the upper limb of it down with the left hand, sliding the eye of the string firmly up, and well into the nock; in doing which, the greatest care must be taken to keep the other three fingers of the

* A backed bow is generally a little reflexed. The bow being thus formed, may deceive, and induce a beginner to imagine, that it is to be bent the way it appears to be inclined, whereas, the proper bending of the bow will be found to be quite the contrary.

left hand away from the string, to avoid the danger of getting them most severely pinched. *See plate* 4. It requires a great deal of practice to be able to string a bow with ease. The young archer, in his endeavour to overcome this first grand point of archery, should always bear in mind, the necessity of never allowing himself to be prompted to pursue any means to effect his purpose, contrary to the rule here offered. Should an archer find himself unable to string his bow, without great exertion, assistance may be given him by another person drawing down the upper horn. After the bow has been strung, the string apparently should run on the bow quite straight from nock to nock. Should the string not appear straight, it may be rectified, by first slackening it, which is effected by pulling the bow up a little with the right hand, and pressing down the upper limb with the left, as in the act of unstringing; and then by twisting the noose with the fore finger and thumb, to the right, or to the left, as may be required.

ON UNSTRINGING.

To unstring a bow. First, grasp it firmly by the handle with the right hand, in the same manner as has been directed for stringing, then place the left wrist so close to the top of the upper horn, that the fore finger may reach round it with ease. Place the tip of the fore finger of the left hand in contact with the eye of the string, then pull up the bow sharply with the right hand, and at the same time, press the upper limb down with the wrist of the left hand. The string being thus loosened, it must instantly be disengaged from the nock, and the thing is done. Regard must be had also to the bend of the bow; therefore, in stringing, experience has taught, that the distance of six inches should be found between the string (that is, from the point of nocking the arrow) and the handle of the bow, *perpendicularly*, or at right angles from the string, for a bow of from five feet six inches, to five feet ten inches in length; but for a Lady's bow, or for a bow not longer than from five feet to five feet two inches, a distance of five inches between the string and the inner part of the handle of the bow will be sufficient. The proper bending of a bow as above recommended, for one of about five feet eight inches or five feet ten inches in length, from nock to nock, may be tolerably well ascertained, by placing the fist *within* the string perpendicularly to the handle. If the thumb when extended, can just touch the handle, the bow may be deemed to be well and properly braced. Should a bow be cast on one side, which will easily be discovered by looking along it when braced, the string should be so regulated, as to lie most on the convex side, which will tend to bring the bow in a single straight line. Indeed, occasional attention should be paid to the string by the archer, during the time of shooting, to guard against the possibility of its getting awry, to the great detriment, and, ultimately, perhaps, to the danger of his bow.

ON THE IMPORTANCE OF GOOD STRINGS.

Nothing in archery is more liable to cause the fracture of a bow, than a bad string; and because an inexperienced archer may easily be deceived in the choice of strings, it is much to be recommended, that the best reputed bowyers be relied on in this particular. When the string begins to wear, "trust it not," says Ascham, "but away with it, for it is an yll saved halfpeny that costes a man a crowne." Many a good bow has been broken through the failure of a string. It has long been thought, that Italian, or Flemish hemp, makes the best strings. The Italian hemp is stronger in texture, and has longer threads than any other. The strings are made of the longest threads twisted tightly, and secured with a sort of water glue,* to guard them against the effects of wet. The eye, or that part of the string, which occupies the upper horn of the bow, is made with the string, and is much thicker than the other part. The other end of the string, is generally loose, in order that the archer may regulate the formation of the noose for the lower horn, according to the length of his bow. The reader is referred to *plate* 4, for a representation of the manner of making the noose for the lower horn. The choice of the string will naturally be, in some degree regulated by the strength of the bow. A thick string will, undoubtedly, be safer for a strong or a backed bow, than a thin one, but it will not allow so quick a cast as the latter. A thick string has the advantage over a thin one, in a greater certainty of shot; but the thin one will cast farther. Upon the whole, it appears that a gentleman's bow of about 60lb. power, should not be strung with a very thin string, particularly if the bow be a backed one, and much reflexed.

OF WHIPPING STRINGS.

Bow-strings should always be whipped either with silk, or fine twine, at the nocking point, and also about the breadth of the fingers used in drawing, both above and below this point. The whipping, as well as the string, should be well waxed, with bees' wax, and thus it will answer the purposes, of securing the bow-string from fret, and of filling the nock of the arrow which should always sit rather tight on the string, than otherwise.

* Roberts's "English Bow-man."

It is the practice of some archers to whip the eye also, and the noose of the string, and a little below each. This is certainly to be recommended, particularly when a string, after two or three day's shooting, has proved itself worthy. The noose, it should be remembered, is much more likely to wear or fret, than the eye of the string; principally from the peculiar mode of its construction.

OF THE HORNS OF THE BOW.

As it has been shewn, that the safety of the bow, depends much upon the security of the string, so it is of importance, that the horns be made smooth, and in such a manner, that the string may pass freely, without danger of being fretted. Roundness and evenness in that part of the horn where the string rests, are indispensably necessary. The centre of both nocks of the horns, is made precisely in the centre of the back of both horns, and each nock brought equally round towards the belly of the bow. Thus, the string upon a straight bow, will run directly, from nock to nock, upon the belly of the instrument. The upper horn is not only larger than the lower, but is often ornamented, a custom that is very ancient.

OF THE HANDLE.

The handle of the bow, should be made nearly round, but rather fuller in its shape, on the outer or back part, as well as on the inner or belly part of the instrument, so as to fill the hand comfortably in the grasp. A covering of shag or worsted lace, answers the double purpose of a firm hold, and an ornament.—The position of the handle, is of much importance.—It has been thought, that the upper part of the handle should be placed about half an inch or an inch *above* the exact centre of the bow. Thus, the lower limb is made so much longer than the upper one; and the reason is, that both limbs should act equally. If the handle were placed so that the upper part of it should be the exact centre of the bow, presuming that the two limbs drew equally, the pressure, when three fingers should be used in drawing, would naturally be most on the lower limb. To obviate this objection, it has been deemed advisable, to adopt the mode of placing the handle about half an inch at least *above* the centre.

Some Bowyers, however, have insisted, that the arrow is best cast from the exact centre of the bow,—and to meet the difficulty of unequalness of pressure, when drawing with three fingers, they have made their bows rather stronger in the lower limbs. The preference must undoubtedly be given to that mode which regulates an equal cast in both limbs, which all the argument or philosophy that can be brought forward on the occasion, can never contradict.

OF THE BRACER.

The bracer, or arm guard, is for the purpose of protecting the interior of the bow-arm, from the strokes of the string, and is therefore generally made of stout leather, of from six to eight inches in length, with two straps and buckles to attach it to the arm. *See Plate* 1. The external part of this implement of archery, should be quite smooth, or polished, in order to allow the string to pass over it freely. A rough surface would not only tend to weaken the shoot, by the string lighting on such an impediment, but might soon put the bow in jeopardy from inevitable fretting, and probably the ultimate breaking of the string. It is therefore advisable that an archer supply himself with a new bracer, as soon as the old one begins to wear, or to get the surface of it repolished.

OF THE SHOOTING GLOVE.

An archer would not be able to bear the sharp loose of the bowstring, when pulled with great strength, without the necessary protection of the shooting glove. The following are the inventions generally used for guarding the fingers from the ill effects of the string; viz. 1st. The *shooting glove*, which consists of fingerstalls fastened to strips of thin leather, and which, passing over the knuckles, are attached to a band that buttons round the wrist. These fingerstalls are sometimes sewed to a common glove. 2nd. The *tab*, a piece of stout flat leather, through which the fingers are let, and which lies on the inside of them, just covering the tips. The best leather for these guards, is cow hide, cut down suitably, dressed and polished on that side which is used outwardly.

OF THE BOW.

The revival of archery, since the days of Ascham, has introduced to the attention of the bow-maker, several sorts of foreign wood, " which," says Roberts, " have been found to make bows that rival, and even excel those of the long-famed yew." This may be true in a certain degree, particularly when applied to the novel and excellent invention and late improvement of the *backed* bow ; but most of these woods are of too brittle a nature to be manufactured into *self* bows—" The long-famed yew," however, must not be given up; it can never yield its *natural* superiority. It has indeed one defect, but that one is common to all other bow woods, namely, an inclination to follow the string. Notwithstanding this, it may fearlessly be asserted, that foreign yew,* if free from knots or pins, stands unrivalled. A yew bow is lighter in hand† than any other, and the wood possesses a toughness and quickness of cast, the combination of which qualities, is not easily to be surpassed.

To an experienced archer, the drawing and loosing of a well made self yew bow, supposing the wood to run perfectly free, and such as had a seasoning of at least *two* years, is QUITE delightful. If a comparison may be allowed, between a self foreign, or indeed a good English *yew* bow, and another, not of yew, imagine the first to be like the handling of silk, whilst the latter is the pulling of the common rough hemp. After having said thus much in favour of a self yew bow, it is to be observed, that amongst the many foreign woods which have lately attracted the attention of the bowyer, the "dark ruby" stands pre-eminent. It is a native of the East, difficult to be obtained, and much prized by bow makers. The "Tulip wood" and "Cocoa wood" the "Thorn Acacia" the "Purple wood," and the "Rose wood,"when backed with fine white hiccory, or hornbeam, make excellent bows. The Laburnam, when well selected, is beautiful to the eye. In its grain, it resembles the feathers of the par-

* The Reader is here referred to the first part of this work, under the head of "Improvement of the Bow from its first Invention," for some observations on the value of foreign yew, as a bow wood, &c.

† The lightest woods possess generally the quickest cast.

tridge, from which circumstance, it is sometimes called "Partridge wood". This with an intervening slip of quick casting wood, and backed with hiccory, will make as good, and as handsome a bow, as an archer need possess. Few backed bows, however, can prove more serviceable, than those manufactured with well seasoned lance-wood,* backed with white hiccory. The shape and length, &c. of bows, are regulated according to the nature of the wood, and other circumstances, of which the bowyer must be the best judge.

Some make their bows bend equally throughout, or in a perfect curve, others leave them rather larger proportionably at the handle, so as to cause the draft or bending of the bow to be from either side of it, gradually to the extremities. This last method is doubtless the best, as it not only produces a quicker cast, but prevents that unpleasant jar in the loosing, invariably to be found in bows with *thin* handles. This should be particularly attended to, in the formation of a self bow.

In forming bows, the staves should always be cut, and not *claved*, (as Ascham directs) and that from the bole or trunk of the tree, by reason of its full growth. The greatest nicety and the best judgment are required in this first operation of bow-making, in the course of which the necessity of leaving a little of the sap for the back part of a self bow, should not be forgotten. It may here be observed, that the self-bows are generally made more *round*, than the backed ones; and this roundness, it is said, makes up in some degree, for a deficiency of quickness of cast. Bow-staves, however, should not be cut very thin, or made into bows, until they have been well seasoned; and the best seasoning is length of *time*, in a moderately warm place. The bow-stave having been *cut* into the required form, the necessary paring or scraping, is proceeded in by

* The belly part of a lance-wood bow, is often dyed of a darkish yellow.

the help of an instrument called a tiller, in order to equalise its draught. For a representation of the "tiller," *see plate* 4, in which, at *figure* 2, the bow is seen placed within the top GROOVE, and drawn to the first notch in the stock, say about 18 or 20 inches. Any inequality in the bending, may thus easily be discovered. When the proper bending of the bow shall have been effected, it may be proved and finished. The length of a gentleman's bow, is usually from 5 feet 8 inches to 5 feet 10 inches, but a lady's bow, is from 5 feet to 5 feet 6 inches, the former varying in power from forty-five pounds to seventy pounds and upwards, the latter seldom exceeding thirty-three pounds or thirty-four pounds.

OF PROVING THE BOW.

By "*proving*" a bow, is meant, the putting of it to the test, before we trust to it; and this is easily done, while in an unfinished state, by shooting in it a short time with heavy arrows, nearly double the weight of those proper for the bow when completed; and afterwards carefully noticing where, if it gives at all, it gives most, and, according to Ascham, "providing for that place betimes, lest it pinch, and so fret." When the bow has been thus tried, and it appears to contain good shooting wood, it should be taken to a trusty and skilful workman to be finished, lest, perchance, a fine stave in an ignorant hand, should be totally ruined.

OF WEIGHING THE BOW TO ASCERTAIN ITS POWER.

After a bow has been proved, it should be weighed, and finished off, and polished. The process of weighing a bow, is best effected by means of a *steelyard, see plate* 5, which will give its weight, or that power which is required to draw it up to the length of the arrow.

DESCRIPTION OF PLATE 5.

A, A fixed upright on which the steelyard B is hooked, with its weight C, which should hang freely. D, an iron stay, or loop fixed to the wall, to keep the end of the steelyard level, and to prevent it rising too high, when the bow is drawn. The bow being placed in the lower hook of the steelyard, a strong cord which runs through the leading block E, near the floor, is hooked on the string at the nocking points; the other extremity having a short stick fixed to it at F, is then pulled till the bow is drawn to the proper distance for its destined arrow, which is indicated either by a scale of inches marked on the upright, or on a tape, one end of which is attached to the bow-string, and the other part at the length required, to the handle of the bow. The weight C is moved backwards or forwards until the end of the steelyard will just rise from its support, when the bow is drawn up sufficiently for the full length of its destined arrow. The notch of the steelyard in which the weight rests, will then indicate the exact power of the instrument. It is usual to mark the weight or power of the bow on its back, close by the handle.

OF ARROWS.

"STELES," or arrows without feathers, or heads, are made of several sorts of wood. The wood generally selected for the sheaf, or

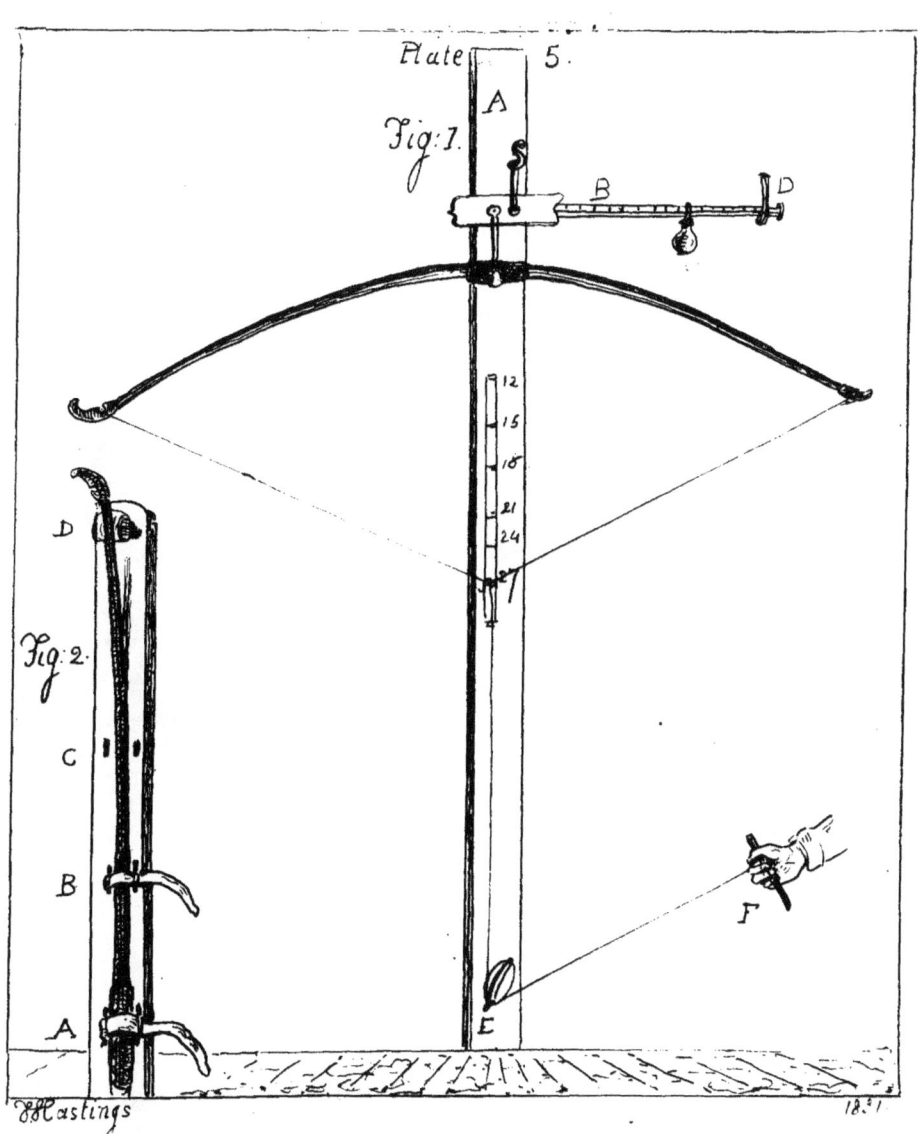

war arrow, was most probably ash. Ascham says, speaking of the war arrows, "it were better to make them of good ashe and not of aspe, for of all other woodes that ever I proved, ashe being bigge is swiftest, and again, hevye to geve a great stripe withall, which aspe shall not do." This writer recommends the mean between the heavy and light woods, being taken for arrow making, such as birch, hardbeam and some ash. He observes, that a stele must be well seasoned, and "made as the graine lyeth, or els it will never flye cleane. A knotty stele is ever in danger of breaking, it flyeth not farre, because the strengthe of the shoote is hindered and stopped at the knot. It is better to have a shaft a little too short, than over long, somewhat too light than over lumpishe, a little too small, than a great deal too bigge." *So is the mean best in all things.* Yet if a man happen to offende in any of the extremes, it is better to offend in want of scantnesse, than in too much, and outrageous excedinge. Let every man when he knoweth his own strengthe, and the nature of every woode, provide, and fit himselfe thereafter. Again, likewise as no one woode can be greatlye meete for all kinde of Shaftes, no more can one fashion of the stele be fit for every shooter." Ascham concludes with the following just remark, respecting the necessity of keeping the shaft *round*. "The shafte must be made rounde, nothing flate, without gall or wemme, for, because roundnesse (whether you take example in heaven or in earth) is fittest shappe and forme, both for fast movinge, and also for soon percinge of any thinge. And therefore *Aristotle* sayth, that nature hath made the raine to be rounde, because it should the easeyer enter through the ayre."

Arrows have lately been manufactured of red deal, asp, and a light white wood of which the Flemish shafts are now generally made, very similar to, and perhaps the same as our Lyme, or Arbele.

The red deal, is with some Fletchers, in high estimation, but as this wood is apt to wear soon and splinter, it is adviseable that the arrows be covered lightly over once or twice with lacker or varnish for their preservation, and which gives a handsome rich appearance to the shaft.* *Lime* is also an excellent arrow wood, its natural heaviness is destroyed by well seasoning, but at the same time, the seasoning renders it rather brittle. Of the proper forms for shafts, it is enough to observe, that those fly farthest and cleanest through the air, which are perfectly round, rather "*high chested*"† or tapering in a *very small degree*, from the shoulder or close to the pile to the nock, taking care that the pile be not heavier than will cause the arrow, when completed, to balance on the finger, about one third or a little more of the way from the pile to the nock, or rather more than half way from the nock to the pile.

OF THE PROPER LENGTHS FOR ARROWS.

Ascham has not noticed the length of the ancient English arrow,—but he says, that at the battle of Agincourt, the army of Henry V, consisted of such archers, that "most part of them drew a yard." Clement Edmonds informs us, that the bow-men under Henry V, did *commonly* shoot with arrows a yard long, "besides the head." Similar facts, says Roberts, have been recorded by Holingshed, Lord Bacon, and also by Carew, and others. But it has been con-

* Mr. Ainsworth of Walton le Dale, near Preston, Bow Maker and Fletcher, makes beautiful and most excellent arrows, and which he covers with thin lacker or varnish. Turkish arrows are often made of deal.

† Arrows if made quite straight would not have substance enough in the chest to stand well in a strong English long-bow.

tended, that at the time spoken of, the cloth yard was only thirty inches. Supposing, however, that the ancient English arrow was a yard, or thirty-six inches long, it must be concluded, that only few bows, if kept to the utmost length, agreeably to the act, could carry arrows of three feet, and that but few archers could draw them to the head. Consequently, as Roberts remarks, the yard of three feet "could not be the *general* standard for the English army, but only for the tallest archers." And it appears from Sir John Smith, that in his time, it was the usual practice for the soldiers to choose their first sheaf of arrows, and to cut those shorter which they found too long for their use. The statute of 5th of Edward IV, directs, "that the arrow be three quarters of the *Standard*." If this *standard* mean three quarters of the English *ell*, then the arrow would be of the length of thirty-three inches and three quarters of an inch; but if it refer to the English *yard*, (as most probably is the case,) then the arrows would be meant to be exactly twenty-seven inches. The arrows generally used in England and Scotland, have, time out of mind, been twenty-seven inches in length, including the pile. It appears, also, from Roberts, that the Leverian Museum contained an *iron* arrow twenty-nine inches long, *including the head*, and barbed, which was dug up some few years ago, near the ruins of Harwood Castle, in Yorkshire. This, in all probability, was a standard arrow for the North. To conclude upon this POINT of archery. It has been a long received opinion, that when a bow is of the length of 5 feet 8 inches, or 5 feet 10 inches between the nocks, the best length for an arrow is twenty-seven inches, and that, *including* the pile. But, as an arrow ought not to be drawn farther than the wood, or to where the pile commences, by reason of the danger of getting the arrow within the bow altogether, which would endanger both the archer as well as the bow, besides inevitably causing the destruction of the arrow, at the moment of loosing, so it appears adviseable, that the arrow should be twenty-seven inches *exclusive* of the pile.* Arrows intended for bows of 5 feet in length, should be twenty-four inches long, *exclusive* of the pile. Some Ladies use bows of 33 and 36 and even 38lbs. power. In such instances, they should be about 5 feet 4 inches in length between the nocks, and the arrows may then be made full twenty-five inches long exclusive of the pile. Flight arrows are made as long as twenty-nine and thirty inches; but drawing these long arrows to the head, with bows having but about 5 feet 8 inches between the nocks, must be always attended with the greatest degree of danger to the bow.

OF THE NECESSARY ATTENTION TO BE PAID TO THE PROPER WEIGHTS OF ARROWS.

Considerable attention was, no doubt, paid by our ancestors, to the weights of arrows, and that the different sorts of arrows, were weighed against each other, or by certain standard weights, there can be no question. A very slight acquaintance with the art of archery, would point out the indispensable necessity and great importance of this nicety. For if an archer, after shooting for some time, (say at the targets when the distance would be limited,) with two arrows of equal weight, should change one of them for another of a different weight, he will immediately find, with equal elevation and loosing, that the heavier of the two, will fall short of, and the lighter one, fly over the mark. By paying attention to the weights of arrows by means of a given standard, many advantages are derived, and one of the greatest is, that it enables the archer to determine instantly, what arrow is best

* Mr. Waring makes his arrows, (for men's bows,) twenty-seven inches in length, *exclusive* of the pile.

calculated, for the bow he intends to use, or for the distance he purposes to shoot. In archery, distance is measured by yards, and this distance is called *length*. By way of scale, generally speaking, for the proper weight of arrows according to the lengths for shooting, it may be said, that an arrow of four shillings weight, would be good for a length of 100 or 150 yards and upwards, and an arrow of five shillings or six shillings weight for a short length of 50 or 60 yards. The above are calculated for men's shooting—The weights of arrows and distances would be proportionably adapted for Ladies. Thus it appears, that the greater the lengths intended to shoot, the lighter should be the arrows, and *vice versa*.

OF WEIGHING ARROWS.

The weights of arrows are marked between the feathers, and an archer, when he sees three shillings or four shillings &c. so placed, knows that such marks denote their weights, and that each weight has been regulated by the standard silver coin of the realm in pennyweights and grains troy.

	dwts.	grs.
The crown piece of the present standard weighing	19	$8\frac{1}{2}$
The half crown	9	$16\frac{1}{4}$
The shilling	3	21

But as the troy weights, from their limited use, may not possibly be so readily understood by some, I have endeavoured, in the following table, to shew pretty nearly, the relative weights of arrows, in centessimals of the ounce avoirdupoise.

Weights of Arrows.		Weights of Arrows.	
By Coin	Centessimals The oz. Avoirdupoise	By Coin	Centessimals The oz. Avoirdupoise
s. d.		s. d.	
. 2 6	. 5437	. 4 10	1 . 0511
. 2 8	. 5799	. 5	1 . 0874
. 2 10	. 6161	. 5 2	1 . 1236
. 3	. 6524	. 5 4	1 . 1598
. 3 2	. 6886	. 5 6	1 . 1961
. 3 4	. 7248	. 5 8	1 . 2323
. 3 6	. 7612	. 5 10	1 . 2685
. 3 8	. 7974	. 6	1 . 3048
. 3 10	. 8336	. 6 2	1 . 3410
. 4	. 8700	. 6 4	1 . 3772
. 4 2	. 9062	. 6 6	1 . 4135
. 4 4	. 9424	. 6 8	1 . 4497
. 4 6	. 9787	. 6 10	1 . 4858
. 4 8	1 . 0149	. 7	1 . 5224

Another table here subjoined, shews the relative value of weights *troy* to the standard or marks for arrows.

Brass Weights Troy.		For Standard Weights or Marks for Arrows.	
dwts.	grns.	s.	d.
—19 .	—— 8½	—5 .	——
—15 .	——12	—4 .	——
—11 .	——15	—3 .	——
— 7 .	——18	—2 .	——
— 3 .	——21	—1 .	——
— 1 .	——22½	—— .	—— 6
	——23¼	—— .	—— 3
	——15½	—— .	—— 2
	—— 7¾	—— .	—— 1

Thus it appears, that if an archer furnish himself with small brass weights agreeably to those laid down in the table, he will be able to regulate his arrows accordingly. For instance, an arrow which weighs 19dwts. 8½grs. will be marked, and consequently called, a "five shilling arrow," and a six shilling arrow will naturally require two weights of 19dwts. 8½grs. and 3dwts. 21grs. to poise it in the scale; and so on.

OF NOCKS OF ARROWS.

The nocks of arrows should be made of horn let into the shaft at the extremity of, and up to the wood in form of a thinly tapered wedge, in which is cut the notch or nock for the reception of the bow-string. The combination of the wood and horn by this method, reduces the liability of the nock being burst by the string. The depth of the nock for the reception of the string, should be made full double the diameter, or thickness of the string, and wide enough only to admit it with a *just* fit. A wide full nock, is apt to let the arrow slip from the string, and missing the loose, may cause the breaking of a shaft to the great danger of the bow. The small nock is best calculated for "clean flying from the hand;" but as it has been observed, "the mean is best in all things," so in this particular, will it be found, that a medium between the large and full nock, and the very small one, will be the safest, and the best for general shooting.

OF THE FEATHER.

"There is no one thinge in all shootinge," says Roger Ascham, "so much to be looked on, as the Feather." This assertion bears with it the strongest conviction, when we reflect, that the grand object in the art of archery, is the accomplishment of the flight of the arrow through the air, with steadiness and velocity. There is no substance in nature so well calculated to assist flight and bear a form through the "liquid air," as the feather. This is sufficiently pointed out to us by the wings of birds; and we know from experience, that with the lightness of the feather, there exists that valuable property of *elasticity*, so particularly essential at the moment of the arrow's passing the bow; for, at the loosing of the arrow, the two under feathers of the shaft, are naturally a little compressed, by coming in contact with it, but the instant that the arrow has passed, the feathers resume their former position, and become the steady wings of flight. The merits of the "*Grey goose wing*," so much celebrated by our historians and poets, may be said to be equalled, or nearly so, by the feathers of the turkey, but certainly surpassed by those of the eagle, as in their superiority of strength and texture, they are much better adapted for the steady flight of the arrow, *particularly when it is sent from a strong bow*. The stronger texture a feather has, the better, provided it be not too coarse. Of a goose's wing, the second, third, and fourth feathers are most esteemed by Fletchers. Feathers for arrows, should not be drawn, but pared with a fine sharp knife, and afterwards cut into proper length and shape for fletching.

Ascham, in his partiality for the "Grey goose wing," and in grateful remembrance to the valuable bird, writes: " Yet well fare the gentle goose, which bringeth to a man, even to his doore, so manye exceedinge commodities. For the goose is man's comfort in warre, and in peace, sleepinge and wakinge. What prase soever is given to shootinge, the goose may challenge the best part in it. Howe well dothe she make a man fare at his table? Howe easilye dothe she make a man lie in his bedde? How fit even as her feathers be only for shootinge, so be her quills fit only for writing. And surely, (said his friend Philologus) that is indede the best prayse you give to a goose yet, and I would have sayde, you had bene to blame, if you had overskipt it."

OF SETTING ON THE FEATHER, AND TRIMMING IT.

Arrows are best fletched with three feathers, set straight on the shaft. One is called the cock feather, which stands uppermost when the arrow is properly "*put in the string*," as it is called, or rightly nocked, and which is generally distinguished by being of a different color, and the other two are so placed, that they may run equally on the bow. The length of the feathers for arrows of about 4s. or 4s. 6d. weight, and twenty-seven inches long, *exclusive* of the pile, should be four inches and a half, or four inches and five-eighths, and set on the shaft about one inch and a quarter, or one inch and three-eighths from the extreme end of the nock; the feather being there at the broadest part, which need not be more than three-eighths of an inch, should be very gradually and finely trimmed to the other end of it. Some fletchers put on their feathers much longer and broader, as the Flemish fletchers do; but it is not necessary, and therefore is rather a hinderance to the flight of the arrow. Should the shaft be a very heavy one, say about 6s. or 7s. weight, then the feathers may be trimmed a little longer and broader, and set on rather higher, and, at the same time, should be proportionably stiffer; also, the *rib*, with which the feather is *pared*, may be a trifle stouter. A Lady's arrow of twenty-four or twenty-five inches in length, and of 2s 6d. or 3s. weight, are fletched with narrower and shorter trimmed feathers. These need not be so stout as the others of 4s. It is a circumstance requiring the greatest attention in fletching, that the three feathers should be either, all from the right wing or all from the left wing, that is, the smooth side should be kept either on the left or on the right hand. And as in the rotary motion of the arrow through the air, the shaft is liable to be much influenced by a side wind, an archer should select from his quiver those arrows suited to the state of the wind, i. e. those which are fletched for the *resistance* necessary on the occasion, to keep the heads true in their proper direction. The resistance of the feather, is to be expected on the convex part of it. Should the arrow afford no resistance by means of the feather, and which would be the case if it ran round *with* the wind, the arrow will naturally be the more influenced in its flight.—By having arrows fletched, some with left, and others with right feathers, an archer is better prepared to encounter a side wind which is one of his greatest obstacles, in shooting.

OF THE HEAD, OR PILE.

The head or pile* of an arrow, is as indispensably necessary as its feathers. A shaft without either, cannot fly to any considerable distance, for with the deficiency of the pile, it will but poorly an-

* Pile appears to be derived from the latin word *pila*, a ball, and was applied to arrow heads belonging to those people who lived within the royal forests in the time of Henry VII, as they were not allowed to shoot with arrows that were not rounded, or *balled* at the heads, on account of the game.—Since this period, the term pile has been indiscriminately given to all sorts of arrow heads.

swer the purposes for which the arrow was originally intended, either, as Ascham observes, "to strike a man's enemye sorer in warre, or to shoote nearer the marke at home." "Heads for warre of longe time hath been made not onlye of divers matters, but also of divers fashions. The Trogans had heades of yron, as this verse, spoken of *Pandarus*, sheweth, "up to the pappe his stringe, did he pull, his shaft to the harde yron." *Iliad* 4.

"The Grecians had heades of brasse, as Ulysses's shafts, were headed with that metal when he slew *Antonius* and the other wooers of *Penelope*. Quite through a door flewe a shaft with a brasse head. Odyss. 21. The men of *Scythia* used heads of brasse. The men of *Inde* used heads of yron. The *Ethiopians* used heads of hard sharpe stone, as both *Herodotus* and *Pollux* doth tell. The *Germaines*, as *Cornelius* Tacitus doth saye, had their shaftes headed with bone, and manye countryes both of old time, and nowe use heades of horne.* But of all other, yron and stele, must needes be the fittest for heades.† Fashion of heades is divers, and that of old time, two manner of arrowes heades, says Pollux, was used in old time." "The one having two pointes or barbes, looking backwarde to the stele, and the feathers, which surelye we call in *Englishe*, a brode arrowe head or a swalowe tayle. The other havinge two pointes stretchinge forwarde, and this *Englishmen* do call a forkeheade. The *Parthians*, at that great battle where they slue riche *Crassus* and his sonne, used brode arroweheades, which stacke so

* The Flemish arrows are at this day tipt with horn, as THEIR laws prohibit arrows being headed with iron or steel.

† The tempering of steel piles for arrows, should be regulated according to the use designed for them. If for piercing wood, the steel must be made to what is called the "*cutting temper*," that is of a pale straw color. If for piercing metal, the steel must be tempered of a much higher color, from which additional heat, it becomes softer, and therefore better adapted for the end proposed. But, for common purposes, the temper of the steel may be managed between these two extremes.

sore, that the *Romaynes* could not pull them out againe. *Commodus* the emperor, used forked-heades, whose fashion, *Herodian* doth lively and naturallye describe, sayinge, that they were like the shap of a newe moone, where-with he would smite the heade of a birde, and never misse. A shaft as long as it flyeth, turns, and when it leaveth turning, it leaveth going any further. And every thing that enters by a turninge and boringe fashion, the more flatter it is, the worse it enters, as a knife, though it be sharpe, yet, because of the edges, will not bore so well as a bodkin."

In plate 6th, are represented, the exact sizes and shapes of three ancient piles, or arrow heads, and also, the shape and size of the bolt of a cross-bow, all which were, a short time ago, dug up nearly under the walls of Carisbrooke castle, in the Isle of Wight.*

In the contemplation of the weights and shapes of these specimens of the English war sheaf arrow's head, and also of the ponderous bolt of the cross bow, we are led to a more ready belief of those accounts which have been furnished us, of the appalling effects produced from time to time by our ancient bowmen, and of the prodigious strength that was required in using such mighty machines.

DESCRIPTION OF PLATE 6.

A, a pile of a war sheaf arrow, weighed in 1828, or although greatly eaten away with rust, and the shaft end broken away, 6 drams (avoidupoise). B, A pile of a lighter sheaf arrow, probably intended for very long shots; and being barbed, this sort of arrow head might have been intended to be used principally against cavalry. This pile, which was also much eaten away, weighed three drams.—

* These relics are now in the possession of Mr. John Dennett, of Newport, in Carisbrooke road. The drawings for the plate were made from the originals.

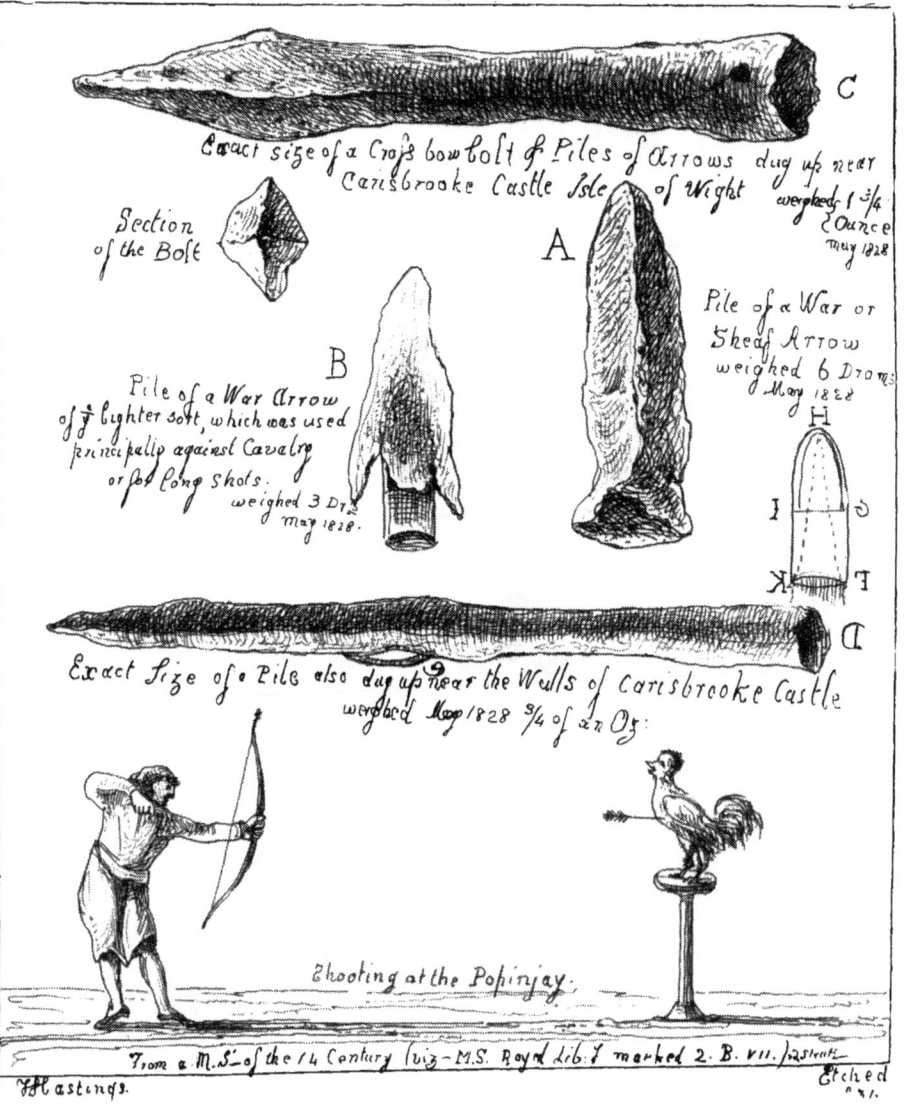

C, a bolt of a cross bow, which also in 1828 weighed $1\frac{3}{4}$ ounce avoidurpoise. D, a pile of a war arrow, supposed to have been intended for carrying fire-works; as at *e* there was a small iron loop evidently, to allow a fastening, and the length of iron from the loop to the shaft, seems to have been intended to guard the wood from the effect of fire. This pile weighed $\frac{3}{4}$ of an ounce. F. G. H. I. K. The round pile of a modern arrow intended for amusement only; in which is shewn the blunt and the sharp point, the latter by the dotted lines, and intended to demonstrate the superiority of the former over the latter particularly against a head-wind.

Arrow heads for the pastime of archery, should be made round, of thin steel, or very hard iron, about $\frac{3}{4}$ of an inch in length, with the mouths just large enough to admit the shaft, after having been scraped a little, or filed sufficiently down from the end, to allow it to go well up to the extremity of the pile, and to fit nicely at F, K; See plate 6.

For shooting in general, and in a calm, an archer will find, that his blunt headed arrows, will fly steadier, and farther than those which are sharp pointed and long tapered; by reason of the rounded heads offering less superficial front of the opposition of the air as it passes through it. The reader is referred to plate 6, where he will find this fact exemplified. At the representation of the arrow head or pile at G, where it is at its extreme breadth, it must be at once evident, that from the point to H, and from H to I, these two lines of front, or of opposition to the air, are much smaller than we find by the two dotted lines from F to H, and from H to K, which in the arrow's passage through the air, must constantly in their *whole* length be opposed to the pressure of it. Yet, long tapered or sharp pointed piles, may be used *with a wind*, or when it blows but a *little* across the shooter, and favourably to the flight of the arrow.

In Roberts's English bowman, is related the fact of " six arrows of equal weight and length, having been constructed with great nicety, three of them had sharp piles, and the other three, had blunt or roving piles. The first three were shot against the latter, several times, the wind being very gentle ; and the result was, that the blunt piles always flew farther than the sharp ones, by about fifteen yards "

OF THE BELT, TASSEL, AND GREASE BOX.

The belt, tassel, and grease box, are necessary articles in an archer's equipment.

The belt is generally made of cow-hide leather, with a stout well or pouch, fixed on the side to receive the pile ends of the arrows, through a leathern loop, which keeps them steady by the side ; and the tassel, which is for the purpose of wiping the dirt from off the arrows, is made of green worsted, and is put on the belt on the opposite side. With respect to the grease box, it may be said, that it should be always considered as a necessary appendage, and the archer would do well in being mindful that it contain a plentiful supply of the grease. This composition, which is made of equal parts of Suet and Bees'-wax melted together, will be found highly useful in keeping the fingers of the shooting glove clean and moist, and will therefore greatly assist the archer in quick and easy loosing. The present mode of carrying this useful article in a neat small mahogany, or some fancy wood box, is very convenient, and is rather ornamental than otherwise at the side of the tassel.

OF STANDING, NOCKING, DRAWING, HOLDING, AND LOOSING.

Standing, nocking, drawing, holding, and loosing, are Ascham's five points of archery. The first point, which embraces not only the mere footing, but the attitude of the archer, requires such attention, Ascham remarks, "as shall be both pleasing to the eye of the beholder, and advantageous to the shooter, setting his countenance, and all parts of his body in such a manner and position, that both all his strength may be employed most to advantage, and his shot made and managed to other men's pleasure and delight. A man must not go hastily about it, nor yet make too much ado about it. One foot must not stand too far from the other, lest he stoop too much, which is unbecoming, nor yet too near the other, least he should stand too upright, for so a man shall neither use his strength well, nor yet stand stedfastly. The mean betwixt both must be kept, a thing more pleasant to behold when it is done, than to be taught how it should be done."

The archer having strung his bow, should place himself in such a manner, that no part of his body be turned towards the mark, but, so that supposing the mark to be due north, his position should be facing directly to the east, which brings the mark immediately on his left,[*] at right angles. Thus placed, and holding his bow horizontally with the string upwards, he takes his arrow by the middle and drawing it from the pouch, carries it *under* the string until the pile pass outside of the left of the bow about an inch, when the fore finger of the left or bow hand, is placed over it, in order to secure the arrow, while the other hand is drawn back to the nock of the arrow, to slide it, with the cock-feather upwards, and so to place the string *well home* in the nock. The nocking, or second point, being now

[*] This is supposing the archer to be a right handed person.

accomplished, the archer secures the perpendicular position of the arrow, by putting his first and second fingers of the right or drawing hand, *close* to, on either side of the nock, and holding it and the string firmly by about the middle of the first joints, now enters upon the third point. Standing erect, with his feet nearly squared, and about eight or ten inches apart he commences the operation of *drawing*, by gradually pressing his bow down firmly with his left hand, at the same time that he draws the string with his right, keeping the right elbow well up, the archer now gracefully raises both arms, his left extended with his bow, which is held with the wrist turned rather inwards, and his right still drawing the string, till the arrow be brought up about half way. The bow being now, we will suppose, sufficiently raised according to the distance of the mark, the archer draws the remainder of the arrow, up to the pile, and keeping his bow firmly fixed, with a moment's aim, which should be sufficient, lets the arrow fly with a steady and sharp loose.*

The steady flight of an arrow, greatly depends on drawing the string evenly, that is, not twisting it, either inwardly or outwardly by the too great exertion of the fingers. Drawing, is one of the nicest points in archery. Ascham considers it to be "*the best part of shooting*." The bow-string is very easily twisted by the joints of the fingers embracing too much of it. It is very common for a young archer to find the arrow turn from his bow, and fall from the string during the time of his drawing, which is caused by his twisting the string; and, if outwardly, it will immediately on the loose, by the recovery of the string, throw the shaft on the side of the bow, and thereby inevitably guide the arrow away from its proper direction, and often cause it to waddle. In target shooting, the drawing

---

* The acts of drawing, holding, and loosing. should be performed as in one movement, so that the archer in taking aim, should not appear to stop or hesitate until the loose be given to his arrow.

is conducted in such a manner, that the nock of the arrow is brought a little under the ear of the archer: but in long shots, as the bow must be more raised, so must the drawing hand be more depressed, and the nock of the arrow is then to be brought down towards the right breast.

Ascham has enumerated all the faults usual among archers, in the following humerous manner.—"Faultes in archers, do exceed the number of archers which come with use of shootinge without teachinge. All the discommodityes which ill custome hath graffed in archers, can neyther be quickly pulled out, nor yet soone reckoned of me, there be so many.—Some shooteth his head forwarde, as though he would byte the marke; another stareth with his eyes, as though they should flye out; another winketh with one eye, and looketh with the other; some make a face with wrything theyr mouth and countenance so, as though they were doinge you wotte what; another, blereth out his tongue; another byteth his lippes; another holdeth his necke awrye. In drawinge, some set such a compasse, as though the would turn about, and blesse* all the field; another maketh such a wrestling with his gere, as though he were able to shoot no more as longe as he live; another, draweth softlye to the middes, and by and by, it is gone you cannot know howe; another draweth his shafte lowe at the breast as though he would shoote at a roving marke, and by and by he lifteth his arme up pricke height; another maketh a wrynchinge with his back, as though a man pinched him behinde; another coureth downe, and layeth out his buttockes, as though he should shoote at arowes; another setteth forwarde his left legge, and draweth back with heade and shoulders, as though he pulled at a rope, or else were afraid of the marke. Another, I saw, which at every shote,

* This alludes to the actions of the Romish Priests in public benedictions; and the passage may explain a very obscure phrase in Spencer, who calls waving the sword in circles, *blessing the sword.*

after the loose, lifted up his righte legge so far, that he was ever in jeopardye of faulinge. Some stampe forwarde, and some leape backwarde. Now afterwarde when the shafte is gone. Some will geve two or three strydes forwarde, daunsinge and hoppinge after his shafte, as long as it flyeth as though he were a madde man. Some, which feare to be too farre gone, runne backwarde, as it were to pull his shafte backe; another runneth forwarde when he feareth to be shorte, heavinge after his armes, as though he woulde help his shafte to flye; another wrythes, or runneth asyde, to pull in his shafte straight. One lifteth up his heele, and so holdeth his foot still, as long as his shafte flyeth." "Now, imagine an archer that is cleane without all these faultes, and I am sure every man would be delighted to see him shoote."

Ascham concludes these remarks, by observing that "standing, nocking, drawing, holding, and loosing, done as they should be done, make fair shootinge."

Observe, that one of the greatest faults an archer can be guilty of, in respect to shooting, is, being unsteady in his bow arm. The arm that holds the bow should be as firm as a gun-stock.

OF SHOOTING AT MARKS.

The archer may proceed to shoot at marks, after he has attained a thorough command over his bow, viz. in bracing and unbracing it, and in the five points of archery just treated on. The shorter the distance, (say from about ten to fifteen yards, which agrees with the Persian method already noticed,) the better for the young archer to commence his practice, and at which, he may in a short time, become so expert, as to hit the smallest mark. Nothing is so likely to prevent a person from becoming an expert archer, as by commencing the practice of shooting at very distant marks.—The bow-arm, and the eye, must in the beginning of the practice of the bow naturally want that steadiness and experience, which can be acquired only by first shooting at short distances.—Without sufficient practice and experience, *long shooting*, can be called nothing else, but *random shooting*. A command over the bow, can be obtained only, by degrees and steady attention. As the young archer finds his improvement, he will be better enabled to increase his lengths to thirty and to sixty yards, which latter has been said to be the key, to all distances within range of the bow. In practising at marks placed at distances from thirty to fifty and sixty, and upwards to one hundred yards, the young archer should always bear in mind, that the best shooting is always the most graceful, because, that which is most graceful is the most perfect; and that it is not enough for him, to be able to *hit* the mark, but, that his hitting should be attended with the utmost steadiness of flight in his arrows. Great advantage may be gained, by practising at the same time at different distances within one hundred yards, which will accustom the archer to various addresses, or degrees of elevation of the bow, necessary for the destined mark. By thus varying the distances, a much greater confidence is acquired in the art of shooting than could ever be attained by keeping to one fixed length. At private, or at public meetings, it is the usual practice to shoot at targets; and the distances commonly adapted, are, for the ladies, fifty or sixty yards, and for the gentlemen one hundred yards.

OF THE VALUE OF HITS ON THE TARGET, &c.

The target or shield to shoot at, is a boss of twisted thrashed * straw, made up in several layers bound very firmly in successive plaits or rows after the manner of a bee-hive. with a flat surface, nearly three inches thick—The targets for ladies are made three feet in diameter, whilst those for the gentlemen are generally four feet in diameter, their fronts are made by coverings of strong sheeting or fine canvass, sewn on the bosses, and of sufficient breadth to preclude the necessity of a joining, and painted in four circles equidistant, besides the gold or centre; viz. the red, inner white, black and outer white, the latter of which is bordered by a green, usually termed the petticoat, or spoon.†

The value of each circle, according to many, is fixed as follows: viz. for,

>The outer white,........one,
>The black,.............three,
>The inner white,........five,
>The red,..............seven,
>And the gold,..........nine,

Although this method may perhaps be said to be rather overrated as to their real value, according to the mathematical division of the target, yet it has been more approved than the actual value of the several circles, which as the gold is usually made a ninth part of the

---

* Thrashed straw is preferable to unthrashed straw, as it makes, in the first place, a firmer boss, and in the next, cannot shrink from frequent piercing in the way that the latter naturally would.

† It was a custom of ancient standing and merriment, that a *horn spoon* should be worn, during the shooting, by whoever last shot his arrow into the *petticoat, or "spoon"*

size of the outer white, the red a third, the inner white, half, and the black only four fifths, will render the respective actual value for the circles, thus; the gold, nine, the red, three, the inner white, two, the black, one and a quarter, or five for four hits, and the outer white one. Ladies' targets, although so much smaller than the gentlemen's, are upon the same principle, and the value of the several circles are reckoned accordingly. Hits on the target, are thus counted, either by the number of them without destinction to the circles, or by number as to their value from the circles on which they may be made.

An account of the game can be kept on a card ruled and marked after the following usual method, and each hit should be pricked with a pin.

Names	Gold 9	Red 7	Inner White 5	Black 3	Outer White 1	Total Hits	Value of
A							
B							
C							

Or, instead of the ruled card, let each archer be furnished with a small *target card*, that is, a card of about two inches and a half in diameter, with the several circles marked and colored thereon similarly to the target. This being suspended, or attached to the left breast of the archer, has an interesting appearance. Every hit should be pricked by a bystander.

Target shooting is generally conducted under the management of one particular archer, who may be styled the "Captain of the Target," and by whom all disputes or differences should be settled. A pair of targets placed opposite to each other, say at the distance of one hundred yards, will do for six gentlemen, and also for as many ladies. Let the whole party of these twelve ladies and gentlemen assemble at one end. The gentlemen will commence shooting, and after having discharged their pouch, or three arrows, they escort the ladies to a mark, or two banners opposite to each other, placed half-way between the targets, from which they will discharge their arrows at the same target as the gentlemen did.

Should the number of archers and archeresses exceed twelve, i. e. six gentlemen and six ladies, it would be adviseable to have other targets, arranged laterally at convenient distances, and each set may be distinguished by a small silk banner, when all the arrows shall have been expended, a simultaneous movement should be made by the whole of the party engaged towards the opposite target.

"Clout shooting," so called, as of old, is when, instead of targets, small pasteboard marks of about a foot diameter, are fixed to a short stick, and stuck in the ground generally from one hundred to one hundred and fifty, and two hundred yards apart. As this sort of mark is small, it is usually arranged, that every arrow counts, that hits, or that falls within two or three bow's lengths of the clout: and this mode of practising in the bow, is adopted by those who may not have *immediate* convenience of a field for targets or butts, but have to resort to a common or distant field, in which case, the inconvenience of conveying these small marks is but trifling.

"Roving,"—is another kind of shooting, attended often with much interest. Any thing, such as a tree, a bush, post, or paling, become fit objects for the archer's attention; and the title of the exercise is derived from the circumstance of the archer's never being necessarily confined to one object. The game and distances are fixed on, as the party proceeds. It is all optional. This kind of shooting appears to be the most ancient of all, and was much attended to when the bow was a national and military weapon.

"Roving," or "shooting at Rovers," as it was called, was much prized by our ancestors. It requires much skill and strength, and a knowledge of distance, which being changed at almost every shot, contributes greatly to the improvement of the archer. Butt shooting formerly was used as roving marks, and not as we now generally shoot at them, as standing marks, without changing the distance at every shot. Butts are made with turfs of earth laid upon each other, and well pressed together, they may be constructed about six or eight feet broad at the base, about six or seven feet high, and of sufficient depth so as to insure stability. Butts are worthy in their construction, if only for their use in saving the trouble of carrying targets and their stands to the ground, for a small pasteboard target may easily be conveyed to the place of exercise, and readily fixed on the face of the butt.

There are other names for different kinds of shooting, such as "hoyle shooting," which, indeed, is similar to "roving:" and "flight shooting," which is only for trying who can shoot the farthest, with various kinds of arrows, and "prick shooting," also, which is nearly the same as target shooting. The ancient "prick mark" was frequently called the *white ;* and probably was a small white pasteboard or piece of white stiff paper put on the butt, the distance for shooting at which, was usually less, than common target shooting.

The Dutch still keep up the ancient game of "the popingjay."*
"It is a mark," says Roberts, "the shape and size of a parrot, which,

*See plate 6.

by these people, is fixed at the top of a high pole, and shot at from the very base of it." The French also practice shooting in the Longbow in a similar manner.

OF TAKING AIM, AND SHOOTING STRAIGHT, AND KEEPING A LENGTH.

"No instrument can be more affected by the animal spirits, than the bow." Coolness, attention, and confidence, should ever be present with the archer; for without these requisites, he cannot expect to attain to any great degree of excellence in his art. Possessed of these, he can take a proper, steady aim; without them, he cannot. At the moment of taking aim, much judgement is required, for the care that is necessary to insure "the keeping the length," is different from that which directs the arrow straight. The first is by the draft and elevation of the bow; the latter is by the eye and mind acting together upon the object of the aim. It should be remembered, that however an archer may find it expedient to give elevation, or otherwise, at the moment of taking aim, (in which he will naturally be directed according to the distance of the mark and strength of his bow,) he should ever accustom himself to keep his eye constantly fixed on the object aimed at. This is indispensably necessary to straight shooting. Ascham particularly insists on this point; he says however, "some, and those very good archers, in drawinge, loke at the marke, untill they come almost to the heade, then they looke at theyr shafte, but at the very lowse, with a second sight, they finde theyr marke againe. This waye, and all other afore of ane rehersed, are but shiftes, and not to be followed in shootinge streight. For leaving a man's eye always on his marke, is the onlye waye to shoote straighte, yea, and I suppose, so redye, and easye a way, if it be learned in youth and confined with use, that a man shall never misse therein. Some men wonder whye, in casting a man's eye at the marke, the hande should go streighte; surelye if he considered the nature of a man's eye, he would not wonder at it. The eye is the verye tongue wherewith witte and reason doth speake to everye parte of the bodye. This is most evident in fencing and feighting. The foot, the hande, and all wayeth upon the eye. The eye is nothing else but a certaine window for wit to shoote out her heade at. The chief cause whye men cannot shoote straight is because they loke at theyr shafte."

Thus it appears from Ascham, (our high authority) and the truth of which may soon be confirmed by experience, that the only advantage to be derived by looking at the shaft head *at the loose*, is, in order for a just elevation, to keep the length, or proper distance of shot; but which as this author justly observes, "yet hindereth excellente shootinge, because a man cannot shoote streight perfectlye, excepte *he loke at his marke*, draw and loose equally, and keep his bow arm steadily and firmly fixed at the time of loosing."

GENERAL OBSERVATIONS, &c.

After every thing that can be said, and all that can be taught, there is still much in the art of archery to be found out and commanded, which theory alone can never accomplish. The bow is an instrument of much simple construction, and therefore its operation and effect depend wholly on the attention and skill of the archer—

Good instruction and example must be backed by practice and an earnest endeavour to excel.

On examination into the history, character, and military career of the English long bow, we may be tempted to conclude, that, from the comparative feebleness of our present archery, the *principles* of the art are lost. But on due consideration, it must be obvious, that there cannot be any material deviation on our part, from those principles which were settled by our ancestors; and that the only reason which can be assigned for our present deficiency in the art of archery, must have arisen from the *partial* attention lately paid to it, and to the want of that constant practice it once had, and which it demands. The art of archery gave birth to sayings, and rise to surnames of existing families—When the demand for implements of archery was universal, the business was conducted or divided into separate branches, from whence arose the names of "Bowyer," "Stringer," "Arrowsmith," "Fledger, or Fletcher," "Pile," "Nock," &c. and amongst other sayings, the well known one of "always have two strings to your bow," evidently by way of admonition to care and prudence. When the names of "Bowyer" "Stringer," &c. were adapted in lieu of, or in addition to others, we must presume that the value of archery was thoroughly felt, and most justly appreciated by the people; for no one would have voluntarily adopted a new name, if the meaning or signification of which had not carried with it a certain degree of consequence and pride. Archery, as has been observed, was the great care of the legislature, and was not only upheld as an art most effective in time of war, but cherished almost to adoration, as a recreative pastime, by all ranks of society among most of the nations of the earth, even in the hours of peace.

OF USING POWERFUL BOWS.

There is no better rule by which a young archer can govern himself in respect to the exact power of the bow which he should first take up, than *judging of his own strength*, at the same time bearing in mind, the absolute necessity of beginning with such a one, as shall be *well within* his power.

By first practising with a suitable instrument, strength, and a command over it, will readily be acquired: then may the weak bow, be changed for a stronger. This method was scrupulously adhered to by the Persians, who trained up their youths to be most excellent archers. Besides it is a fact, that nothing is more likely to deny the chance of any person's becoming a good archer, than first using a bow *fully* equal to, or beyond his strength. This too common and fatal practice has often been attended with very serious consequences, such as, overstraining the muscles of the breast and arms, and more especially the tendons of the drawing hand. The surgeon's knife has been known to be necessary in a recent case, wherein the tendons of the inside of the palm of the drawing hand, had been overstrained, and which produced serious inflammation! Young people, and boys between the ages of ten and fifteen years, may generally be supposed to be able to begin shooting with bows of about thirty pounds or thirty-two pounds power. Those between the ages of sixteen and twenty, may not find bows too strong to commence with of about forty pounds, or forty-five pounds power. Bows of twenty-four or twenty-six pounds will *generally* be found at first to be suitable for ladies of between sixteen and twenty years of age. One or two changes at most, will probably bring an archer or an archeress to be able to draw a bow from the above weak powers, to between twenty-eight pounds, thirty pounds, and forty pounds, for the ladies, and to about fifty pounds, fifty-five pounds, sixty pounds, and seventy pounds for the gentlemen. It may be here observed, however, that for target shooting of the present day, a bow of sixty pounds power, generally speaking, will be found a good standard for gentlemen after having shot with weaker ones a season or two.

OF BREAKING BOWS.

A bow is often broken, either by the giving way of the string, by crooked stringing, by insecure nocking, by the breaking of a shaft, also by frets and crysals, as well as by using too long arrows. When the string breaks in the act of shooting, the bow in recovering itself, receives a sudden and very violent jirk, particularly at the handle, which in the recoil backwards, or against the proper bending of the bow, is raised up; this contrary action, puts the bow in imminent jeopardy. It therefore behoves an archer to be extremely watchful over his string, which, at the instant he perceives in the least degree deficient, even by the rupture of a single thread, should be cast away. The reluctance to take off a string that has served well, and for a cause apparently so trifling, may be natural, but the doing of it would most probably be rewarded in the preservation of a valuable bow.

1st. By crooked stringing.—By this is meant, when the string does not go from the centre of each nock, and consequently, cannot run apparently straight along the belly of the instrument. Such an inaccuracy is easily remedied, by pressing that end of the bow down, which may be necessary, as is done in the act of stringing, and by pressing the loop or noose of the string a little to the side required, AS HAS BEEN NOTICED UNDER THE HEAD OF "*stringing.*"

2ndly. By insecure nocking.—On well nocking, often depends the safety of a bow, as well as of the arrow; for, should the string not be well home in the nock, at the time of loosing, the force of the loose, may readily burst the nock. This violence is apt to give a twist to the string, and consequently to the bow, so as to throw them in their return, out of their straight course, which, in a backed bow particularly, is very likely to cause a fracture.

3rdly. By the breaking of a shaft.—The above observations, on "insecure nocking," are applicable to the present subject.—4thly. By frets and crysals.—It may easily be conceived, that as frets arise from the fibres of the wood giving way at the weaker parts of bows, so in the increase of the evil, (which most probably will be the case in the use of the bow,) if not either worked out, or bandaged up, the dissolution of the instrument, will sooner or later infallibly take place. The same may be remarked respecting "crysals." Frets are most commonly discovered on the backs of bows, and generally arise from positive imperfections in the wood; while crysals, so called among archers, are signified by pinches of the wood, in the bellies of bows, and which, like frets, too frequently prove fatal to the expectations of the archer. A crysal is caused by the fibres of the wood, being bent *inwards*, and pressed into one another, as it were at their several disjunctions. A crysal generally increases in magnitude with the use of the bow, until the destruction of the instrument takes place. Sometimes indeed a bandage timely applied, will prevent the mischief of a crysal or fret from further spreading. Fibres are liable to be disjointed in the working of the wood. The cure of these diseases of bows, should be attempted to be cured, only through the advice, or by the assistance of *an able surgeon*, or, in other words, by a skilful bowyer. As the breaking of a bow may be attended with serious consequences, to a bystander, it is to be recommended, that no one should stand in advance of the shooter, as fragments of a broken bow will sometimes fly to the distance of 15 or 20 yards, which must naturally imply sufficient force to knock out an eye, or wound a person in the face. A deep scratch in a bow may very soon cause a fret, to the ultimate ruin of the instrument. A bow must be always drawn in the middle, as by pulling the string too high or too low, it necessarily follows, that the then shorter limb is overstrained, which may endanger it. Shooting should be avoided in frosty weather; for then the sap expands, which renders a bow unfit for service; while in warm weather, the sap, the soul of the instrument, collapses, and fits the bow for action. Moist weather is also unfriendly to bows, as well as to arrows.

OF PRESERVING BOWS.

A good bow is deserving of every attention. It requires nearly as much care as a fine violin, or any other delicate musical instrument. It should be rubbed well occasionally with flannel, or with fine woollen cloth and a little bees' wax, particularly after shooting, and kept in an oil cloth, lined with baize, in order to preserve it from damp, or from moist weather. The fashion of the day, among bowyers, is to finish their bows, with a high French polish. It is unquestionably a very attractive one, but perhaps not very advantageous to the wood, as to preserve a bow in the best way, is by rubbing it well with " cold drawn" or raw linseed oil about once a year, at the termination of the shooting season—As there is no doubt of raw linseed oil proving thus useful either to a backed or to a self bow, the benefit thereof, is at once denied by the superficial texture of the French polish, at the same time it may be observed, that there can be no objection to the French polish provided it be taken off the bow every year or two, to allow the instrument being rubbed with the linseed oil;—after which the French polish may be renewed with benefit. It should be remembered, that yew, which from its nature, is of so long duration, that it does not require oil in the same proportion that other bow woods do; and yew will absorb oil faster than any other bow wood that is known. Hence, the necessity of using oil on a bow of this description, but sparingly. Bows should be kept in a *temperate* room, but not against a stone wall as it attracts damp. The best method of keeping bows, is in a cupboard designed and kept solely for the purpose of containing all the implements of archery. Such a cupboard is called by archers, an "*Ascham*"* and has derived its name from the great advocate and writer on archery. The precaution of unbending a good bow during the time of shooting, is unnecessary, but the bow should always be unstrung after the shooting is over.

As it is natural for all wood to incline or follow the bending, which relative to bows, is termed "*following the string*," I have invented and adapted a "bow stock" after the following simple method, and which has been found highly serviceable. The bow stock, see fig. 2. plate 5. is a plain piece of deal about 6 feet. 3 inches long, $2\frac{1}{4}$

---

* An " Ascham" should be made about seven feet high i. e. in the "clear" within. About thirty inches from the base upwards, it is made broader outwards, for the purpose of receiving a rack with holes pierced and fixed horizontally, to hold a few dozen arrows, as may be convenient; over this broader part is a flap, which covers the arrows, and from which upwards the door of the "Ascham" is placed. The bows are arranged at the back, having a free space between them and the racks of a few inches, and may be held in their places by small straps of leather, on brass knobs.

inches broad and 2 inches thick. Two small strap holes opposite each other are cut, about 3 feet from the bottom, and so far separated as to allow the handle of the bow to rest between them. Two other sets of strap holes are also cut at certain distances say at a foot, and at 18 in. from the centre, as at B, and C. *for one half* of the bow stock, and corresponding ones, for the other half. Instead of giving the bow a reversed sharp action after shooting, for the purpose of putting it in its wonted position, as is commonly the practice, place it on the bow-stock with the back upwards, or belly against the stock, brace it closely at the handle as at A, and moderately so at either of the other places for strapping as may be found necessary. Then the ends of the bow may be raised and fixed in a moderately reflexed position, by large pieces of cork, keeping the bow thus on the bow-stock for a few hours, will be found extremely serviceable, and be the safest method that can be adopted towards preserving its proper shape.

OF THE TILLER.

The tiller, (No. 1, in plate 4,) is an instrument used in bow making, for regulating the bending of the limbs of the bow.

In the constant care necessary for the preservation, or for the well keeping of the bow; the tiller may be found very useful. New bows, particularly self ones, generally demand some trifling scraping for the sake of relief to one or both the limbs, after having been shot in a few months. In plate 4, No. 2, a bow is represented placed in the tiller, and drawn as far as may be necessary to the first, second, third, or fourth notch, each notch made at the several distances of eighteen, twenty, twenty-four, and twenty-seven inches. Thus any irregularity in the bending of the bow, may be readily seen, and soon rectified; and such an instrument may be nearly as serviceable to the archer, as to the bowyer. Without very great care, however, it might prove more advantageous to the latter than to the former, as a bow may be soon ruined by injudicious scraping!

FEATS OF MODERN ARCHERY.

The anecdotes of archery which have been given, in the preceding part of this work afford sufficient proof, that the bow in the hands of numbers, was a most effective and terrible weapon. It has long been laid aside as a weapon of war, therefore it cannot be expected, that such extraordinary feats as at one time supported its consequence, can be authenticated by occular proof in the display of our modern archery, as for many years past the bow has been used merely as an instrument of polite amusement.

From the experience which an archer of the present day acquires, after a practice of one or two years, a tolerable accurate judgment may be formed, upon the truth of the recorded facts of our ancient archery; and while it may readily be owned, that the common range of the long war-bow was, in the hands of strong athletic men, from eighteen to twenty score yards, at which distances, showers of arrows were often poured down in succession upon the enemy's ranks with dreadful effect, yet it is impossible for experience to allow credulity to carry us away so far, as to credit those marvellous feats mentioned in the ballads of Robin Hood and other ancient stories, such as shooting an arrow from the long-bow to the distance of a mile and sometimes farther!!

Stuart, in his *Antiquities* of Athens, vol. 1, p. 10, mentions a shot, from a Turkish bow made by Hassan Aga in the year 1753, to have been five hundred and eighty four yards and one foot, English measure.—Cantimir, *in his History of the Ottoman Empire*, speaking of the Emperor Murad IV, says, "In the art of shooting with the bow, he had not his equal in the whole Turkish nation, except the famous champion Tozcoparan. There are now two marble pillars standing *fifteen hundred cubits* asunder, over which he is said to have shot an arrow."

Roberts, in his work on archery, records that in the year 1795, Mamhood Effendij, secretary to the Turkish ambassador, a man possessing very great muscular power, shot an arrow from a Turkish bow, *four hundred and eighty-two yards*, in the presence of three gentlemen, of the Toxophilite society, now living, who measured the distance, and to whom he observed, that his emperor, Sultan Selim, could shoot further than any one of his subjects. In the year 1798 the Sultan exhibited a proof of his strength and skill in archery, by shooting, in the presence of Sir Robert Ainslie, late ambassador to the Ottoman Porte, an arrow, *fourteen* hundred pikes Turkish measure, or, *nine hundred and seventy-two yards, two inches and three quarters*, English measure, and which distance was measured in the presence of Sir Robert Ainslie.—Mr. Roberts adds, that the arrows used by the Turks, for very long shots, do not exceed twenty six inches in length, but they are drawn several inches within the bow, in a grooved horn, used for the occasion: they are tapered from the nock to the pile,* which is exceedingly small, and weigh about three shillings and two pence English arrow weight.

It appears also from Roberts, that a Mr. James Rawson, who died about the year 1794, "the best archer of his day," shot an arrow *eighteen score yards*. And in 1798, Mr. Troward, a member "of the Toxophilite society, shot on Mousley Hurst, *seventeen score yards;*" and it is well recorded that this was not an accidental shot made by Mr. Troward, but that he *repeatedly* shot that distance during the same day, in the presence of many other members of the society; and further, that as his shots were made during a contest for a prize, each was measured with the greatest possible accuracy; and the field was marked or staked out in scores, and half scores. Mr. Troward shot with a *self* bow, of sixty-three pounds power; his arrows, were *twenty-nine* inches in length, and about four shillings weight.—The bow with which Mr. Rawson shot, was a *backed* one."

All the appearance of undoubted veracity is certainly stamped on the above records of these feats of modern archery. I have often seen arrows from bows of about sixty and sixty-three or four pounds power, pierce through the deal legs of a large target-stand, which were full one inch and a quarter thick, at one hundred yards distance: and I have myself frequently pierced a large target quite through, and the pile of the arrow which was an inch long, has often nearly buried itself in the stand behind the target, shooting the distance of one hundred yards. From twelve to fifteen score yards, may be esteemed a good *modern* flight for an arrow, twenty-

---

* This practice of the Turks, presuming that it was founded upon experience, seems as to the philosophy of the matter, in direct variance with the fact recorded in the former part of this book, under the subject of "Heads or piles of arrows," viz. that, some blunt headed arrows, in an experiment made between such and some sharp headed ones, always flew the furthest.

eight inches long including the pile, and about 4s. weight, shot from a bow of sixty or sixty-two pounds power. Early and constant use will give great power to the muscles of the body. This fact is so well and generally known, that there needs no evidence for the support of it. When therefore we read of armour being pierced through and through, and that the stoutest and best tempered steel that could be procured, and worn in the field, proved but a weak defence against the execution of the ancient English arrows, and that by the great force of them, helmets, lances, and swords, were literally *battered, and split in pieces*, what an amazing idea it immediately creates, of the muscular strength that must have been acquired in the constant exercise of the long-bow. It conveys notions of power not to be found, but through mechanical means. A little reflection however on the effect of habit, and training the body from early youth to all sorts of fatigue, will induce us to extend our conception of muscular strength, to a much greater degree, than might at first appear reasonable.

CONCLUSION.

The FINE or POLITE ARTS, considered in their full scope, may be said to comprise all arts and sciences that tend to ameliorate the conditions of social life, and to increase social happiness; and in contemplating this fact, it appears that the art or, as it has been called, the pastime of archery stands eminent, which by a mute, yet unoffending influence, peculiar to itself, powerfully tends to rational pleasure, and therefore may be allowed to keep pace with other means of general improvement. Whatever informs and refines the intellect of man, or whatever assists or strengthens the inclination after any object, or the improvement of any pursuit, by way of recreation, must, in the same proportion, diminish his grosser conceptions.—All arts and recreative pastimes innocent in themselves, contribute to impress happy and lively impressions on the soul, which become a security against the rankness of error and of vice, and may soon convert the *wilderness* mind into a wholesome *garden*, in whose soil, virtue makes her strongest shoots, and *politeness* blossoms into *humanity!*

The pursuit of archery, as an object of recreation and amusement, tends, in conjunction with other resources, to produce, and to increase the invaluable blessing of health. If the body be healthy and vigorous, it is a great point gained towards the improvement of a genuine cheerfulness of heart, and a lively cheerfulness of heart is the sunshine of life, for it imparts its felicity to all around. Even an indifferent temper may be improved, by exercise in the field with an object in view, and with that content of spirit which naturally springs from a well regulated intercourse with friends in the mutual enjoyment of such exercise. This life was never intended by our benevolent Creator, to be one of gloom, and desert existence, but on the contrary: by mutual good-will and friendly feeling to one another, that it should always prove an effectual source of cheerfulness and contentment.—In this great commercial country, a cold reserve and selfish spirit, the parent of every meanness, too frequently usurps the throne of the heart, to the destruction of higher and more noble sentiments. The better the society the more enlightened and liberal should be the sentiments of its members;—Affectation of greatness, assumption of consequence, and singularity of notions, which would oppose frequent meetings of both sexes on the target ground, are not known in true gentility.

We naturally look to the society of ladies, for every thing that can endear the common scenes of life; they enhance the pleasures of general association: there is necessarily a blank without their enlivening presence, they are our homes, and who could debar them from the recreative pastime of archery, or encourage the absurd idea, perchance entertained by a few curiously minded persons that this elegant amusement savours too much of masculineness? Whenever it may be agreeable to ladies to join in the exercise of shooting in the bow, surely it should be esteemed by the archers, as an opportunity of doubling the pleasures attendant on the pursuit.

It is a pity that amidst the rigidity of business, or professional avocations, various recreations, in the shape of accomplishments, are not more frequently cultivated, if only for the purpose of relieving the burdened mind! Those *persons* who have resources within themselves, know full well their respective blessings, and surely they would be the last to exclude the Fair from any amusements, consistent with the sex; for the natural wish that attends the possessor, while in the enjoyment of any accomplished pursuit is, *that every one might taste of the same fruit*. Business, then could hardly be a dreary toil, but would be metamorphosed, as it were, into another pleasant resource, and the *"utile cum dulci"* be established; and as accomplishments are highly valuable, it appears reasonable to conclude, that those recreations which require attendance in the open air, must above all others be particularly desirable.

The arts of drawing and of painting are inestimable, and sketching and painting from nature, afford two of the richest treats that can be imagined or enjoyed.

The art of archery, that delightful energetic exercise, which, as has been observed, is never necessarily laborious, is in its particular pursuit, calculated to inspire benevolence towards each other, as it is never attended with petty jealousies, or *a thirst of honorably robbing from another's purse*; and it is in its own peculiarity, too open to admit a meanness. Archery furthers all good associations, and true hearty fellowship.

Let therefore a wish be cherished in the breasts of those who have it in their power, to promote both friendship, and happy pastimes as have been just alluded to: I shall now conclude with Hargrove, in his anecdotes on archery, respecting the alteration of the ancient dreadful long bow as a weapon of destruction, to an implement of peaceful recreation, and hope, that every instument invented for the destruction of man, may share the same fate, and that those happy days may soon arrive, which are thus so well described.

> "No more shall nation against nation rise,
> Nor ardent warriors meet with hateful eyes;
> Nor fields with gleaming steel be cover'd o'er,
> The brazen trumpets kindle rage no more;
> But useless lances into scythes shall bend,
> And the broad falchion in a plow share end."

A GLOSSARY

OF THE TERMS COMMONLY USED IN ARCHERY.

A.

Arrow Sheaf, a war arrow, twenty-four of which would constitute a Sheaf of Arrows.
Ascham, a Cupboard or Case to contain bows and arrows and other implements of Archery.

B.

Back of a bow, the exterior.
Belly of a bow, the interior.
Bow shot, the distance which an arrow flies from the bow.
Brace, to bend a bow.—A bow may be too much or too little braced.
Butt, a mound of earth whereon to place a mark.

C.

Cast, signifying *warped*, and used to a bow of quick or slow *cast*.
Crysal or Chrysal, a kind of pinch, (in appearance like the fret of a worm,) in a bow.
Clout, a small target.
———, clout shooting, shooting at clouts.
Cock feather, that which has no one parallel to it.
Come round Compass, a bow is said to "Come round Compass" when it forms a proper curve in drawing.
Compass, to shoot Compass or a round Compass, is to shoot the arrow in a curved or parabolic line.
Cut, an arrow *cuts* the mark when it flies straight to it, but falls *under* it.

D.

Dead shaft, a heavy dull one.
Drawing the string, an act which immediately precedes the loosing.
Drawing thro' the bow, when the point of the arrow comes beyond the belly of the bow.
Drawing a feather, slipping it from the quill.

E.

Elevation, raising the bow to the mark.
Eye of the string, that part which occupies the upper horn of the bow.

F.

Fast, a word formerly used to stop a person when proceeding between the shooter and the mark, inattention to which would exonerate the archer in case of accident.
Fletcher, an arrow maker.
Following the string, is when a bow by use has lost somewhat of its original straightness.
Fret, the part of the wood eaten or cracked away, and signifies also that rising occasioned by the bow being strained.

G.

Gall, see Knot-gall.

H.

Holding, the act of holding the string, when the bow is drawn up.

I.

Inches, or distance allowed the butt mark, in which an arrow must fall in order to count.

K.

Keeping a length, to shoot the exact distance.
Knot-gall, a hurt in trees, occasioned perhaps by boughs growing or rubbing against the part.

L.

Length, the distance intended to be shot.
Limb of a bow, that part which extends from either side of the handle to the horns.
Low-feathered, when an arrow's feathers are cut *short* and *shallow.*

N.

Nock, the ancient word for *notch*, which by archers is still used; and to nock, is to "place the nock of the arrow in the string," but perhaps with more correctness, should be said, to place the string in the nock of the arrow.

Noose, that end of the string which is fastened at the *lower* horn.

O.

Over-bowed, when an archer's power is not sufficient for his bow.

Over-hand, shooting over hand, is to look at the mark *over* the bow hand.

P.

Petticoat or Spoon, the ground of the target beyond the outer white.

Pinch, a small fret.

Popinjay, a mark like a bird.

Prick mark, the white mark shot at.

Prick shooting, shooting at prick marks.

Pile, the head of an arrow, used indiscriminately for all heads of arrows.

R.

Rovers, casual marks.

Roving, shooting at rovers.

S.

Set, the Shaft in the bow, so that in pulling, the arrow gets beyond the belly of the bow, and touches it in its return.

Shaft, an arrow wanting the head only.

Shaftment, that part of the arrow whereon the feathers are placed.

Shake, a longitudinal crack, often caused by the wind or weather, or by the bow or wood being kept in too dry or hot a place.

Sheaf, of Arrows, a Quiver or Case of twenty-four in number.

Shoot, an arrow shot.

Sinking a bow, reducing the spirit or stiffness of it.

Snake, an arrow is said to snake, when it buries, or works itself under the grass.

Spell, a rising of the grain of the wood.

Spoon, see petticoat.

Stand, an arrow stands in the bow, if it be placed so as to fly from it steadily.
Stele, an arrow without feather or head.

T

Tab, a piece of flat leather used instead of shooting gloves.
Target, a mark to shoot at, consisting of circles.
Target-card, used in scoring when shooting at the targets, formed like unto the targets with the several circles coloured.
Tiller, an instrument used in altering a bow. It has a large notch at the top of it to hold the handle of the bow, and small notches on the upper side to place the string in, when trying the bow previous to scraping it.
Tillering, trying the bending of a bow by the tiller.

U.

Under-bowed, when an archer uses a bow that is too weak for him to shoot well with.

W.

Weight of a bow, or power which it requires to draw it up to the length of the arrow destined for it.
Wind down, which blows from the shooter directly to the mark.
Wind up, which blows from the mark to the shooter.
Wind side, when it blows across the line of the mark.
Wide arrow, so called, when it falls wide of the mark.

INDEX.

PART I.

	Page.
The introduction of Archery, and high consequence of the art to the early hunter and warrior	1
On the invention of the bow	3
On the improvement of the bow from its first invention, &c.	5
Anecdotes of Archery, from various high authorities, with some account of Robin Hood	13
Dress of an Ancient English Archer, &c.	57
Observations on the utility of the bow as a weapon of war	58

PART II.

Archery, valuable as an amusement	66

PART III.

The art and practice of Archery	71
On Stringing—and particular attention to be paid to the bow when strung	72
On unstringing, &c.	73
On the importance of good strings, and different effects of thick and thin strings	74
Of whipping bow strings	75
Of the horns of the bow	76
Of the handle	76
Of the bracer	77
Of the shooting glove	78
Of the bow—choice of and lengths of &c.	78
Of proving the bow	81
Of weighing the bow to ascertain its power	82

INDEX.

	Page.
Of arrows	82
Of the proper lengths for arrows	84
Of the necessary attention to be paid to the proper weights of arrows	86
Of weighing arrows—with tables shewing the relative weights of arrows in centessimals of the ounce avoirdupoise, and the relative value of weights troy, to the standard or marks for arrows	87
Of nocks of arrows	89
Of the feather	89
Of setting on the feather, and trimming it	91
Of the head or pile	92
Of the belt, tassel, and grease-box	96
Of standing, nocking, drawing, holding, and loosing	97
Of shooting at marks	100
Of the value of hits on the target, &c. and different kinds of games of shooting	102
Of taking aim, shooting straight, and keeping a length	106
General observations	107
Of using powerful bows	109
Of breaking bows	110
Of preserving bows	112
Of the tiller	114
Feats of modern archery	115
Conclusion,	118
Glossary	125

YELF, PRINTER, NEWPORT, ISLE OF WIGHT.

www.ingramcontent.com/pod-product-compliance
Lightning Source LLC
Chambersburg PA
CBHW070917160426
43193CB00011B/1503